"Koreen's experience, knowledge, and insight in designing learning environments shine through in this work through impactful storytelling and wonderful metaphors. She provides vivid case studies, conversational explanations, and enough encouragement to convince you that immersive learning is not only the correct instructional approach, but also that you can and should get started immediately."

—Karl M. Kapp
Professor of Instructional Technology, Bloomsburg University
Author of *The Gamification of Learning and Instruction*

"*Immersive Learning* is the first book to take the notion of learning experience, flesh it out, and map it to new technologies such as virtual worlds and augmented reality games. Illustrated with illuminating examples and insightful heuristics, this book provides a practical road map to designing and developing such experiences. Mixing good learning principles, engaging design concepts, and hard-won lessons, Koreen Olbrish Pagano has laid out a compelling and practical guide to the future of learning."

—Clark Quinn
Author of *Designing mLearning: Tapping Into the Mobile Revolution for Organizational Performance*

"The American theoretical physicist Richard Feynman once said, `What I cannot create, I cannot understand.' Creation is a common theme in *Immersive Learning*: creating practice opportunities, creating emotional connections, creating learning environments, and creating productive interactions. While recognizing the role of technology to reduce uncertainty in goal-driven activities, this book never loses sight of what makes learning genuinely (and personally) rewarding: a sense of fun and wonderment on the part of the student. The author's evident enthusiasm for her subject matter leaps from these pages. She cites numerous case studies in both evidence-based and incentive-based learning, providing readers the tools they need to endorse their application to any learning context."

—Kel Smith
Principal of Anikto LLC
Author of *Digital Outcasts*

"*Immersive Learning* is a manifesto for the future of learning design. It emphasizes the need to do instructional design differently to change the nature of learning design's impact on the organization. The case studies provide concrete examples to show that it can be done with phenomenal results. Read *Immersive Learning* and begin using designed practice to turn your content into behavior change."

—Andy Petroski
Director and Assistant Professor of Learning Technologies
Harrisburg University of Science & Technology

IMMERSIVE LEARNING

Designing for Authentic Practice

Koreen Olbrish Pagano

ASTD Press is an internationally renowned source of insightful and practical information on workplace learning, performance, and professional development.

ASTD Press
1640 King Street Box 1443
Alexandria, VA 22313-1443 USA

Ordering information: Books published by ASTD Press can be purchased by visiting ASTD's website at store.astd.org or by calling 800.628.2783 or 703.683.8100.

Library of Congress Control Number: 2013951484
ISBN-10: 1-56286-821-7
ISBN-13: 978-1-56286-821-5
e-ISBN: 978-1-60728-643-1

ASTD Press Editorial Staff:
Director: Glenn Saltzman
Manager, ASTD Press: Ashley McDonald
Community of Practice Manager, Learning Technologies: Justin Brusino
Senior Associate Editor: Heidi Smith
Editorial Assistant: Ashley Slade
Cover Design: Mazin Abdelgader
Interior Design and Layout: Natasha Van De Graaff, Ana Ilieva Foreman, and Marisa Kelly
Printed by: Versa Press, East Peoria, IL, www.versapress.com

CONTENTS

DEDICATION

For my kiddos—Clarisse, Elvis, Jackson, Vardan, Sallie Rose, and Zevon—who immerse me in learning every day, and for my mom, who always told me I could be anything I wanted to be.

INTRODUCTION

In my favorite *South Park* episode, there is a mysterious problem: All of the boys' underpants are being stolen every night. The parents are angry; they can't understand why all of their children's underpants are disappearing.

The boys stay up one night to try to catch the underpants thieves, and discover that the culprits are gnomes. Following the gnomes (who are carrying more stolen underpants) through a hole in the wall and into their underground cavern, they find enormous rooms, full of all of the kids' underpants that they had been stealing.

The boys confront the gnomes, and ask why they are stealing the underpants. The gnomes explain:

WHY GNOMES COLLECT UNDERPANTS

Phase 1	**Phase 2**	**Phase 3**
Collect Underpants	?	Profit

The problem is, of course, what is "Phase 2"?

We have the same problem with learning. We collect information—aka content—and provide it to learners. Then we make the mysterious leap to Phase 3: in our case, behavior change.

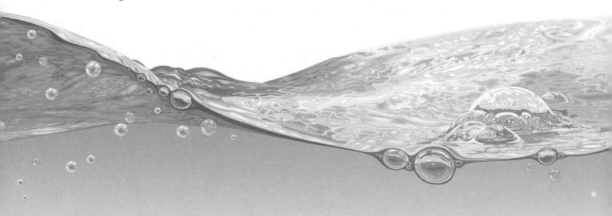

```
TRAINING PHASES

    Phase 1      Phase 2      Phase 3
    _____

    Content         ?         Behavior
                              Change

    What is Phase 2 for training?
```

Does it work? Does providing information to learners lead to improved performance and behavior change? Sometimes, maybe yes. Often, probably not. Just because I know something doesn't mean I can do it. I know how other people ride a skateboard; I can't do it myself. I've watched great web developers create amazing interactive experiences, but I don't have the expertise to model that even if I can see the source code. What would give me the skills to improve my performance? Practice. How do we create practice opportunities? We design them.

```
COMPLETE TRAINING PHASES

    Phase 1      Phase 2      Phase 3
    _____

    Content      Designed     Behavior
                 Practice      Change

    Does your organization's curriculum include Phase 2?
```

Phase 2 for learning professionals is designed practice. Some people may have answered the Phase 2 question differently; they may have proposed technology as the mysterious Phase 2, as if technology is somehow the magical conduit of content, the bridge from content presentation that leads to behavior change. When I'm asked to present on the future of learning technology, or on emerging technology trends, I always come back to the same argument: The future of learning technology has very little to do with the technologies. Technology is a tool, an enabler, a facilitator of achievements—but it is just a tool. It is how you use the tool that makes it effective. Design is what differentiates our experience; it makes things easier to use, more meaningful, more efficient, and more fun. Design leveraging technology helps facilitate your goals, but it is not the technology itself that creates the experience. Technology creates opportunities; design activates them.

The future of technology-enabled learning is mobile, augmented, visual, location-based, kinetic, and story-line driven. The future of technology-enabled learning is immersive. Immersive in the sense that I am "in" the learning experience and I am practicing doing the things that I need to do better. I am making decisions. I am leading a team. I am operating a medical device. I am interviewing for a job. I'm practicing and I'm getting real-time feedback and I'm getting better. Technology allows that to happen anytime, anywhere.

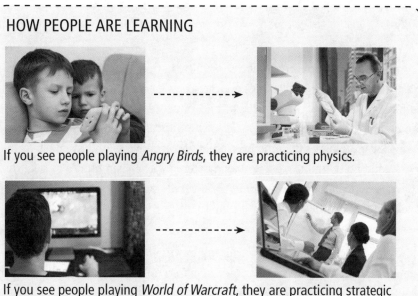

HOW PEOPLE ARE LEARNING

If you see people playing *Angry Birds*, they are practicing physics.

If you see people playing *World of Warcraft*, they are practicing strategic planning, team building, and leadership skills.

Graphics courtesy of Shutterstock.

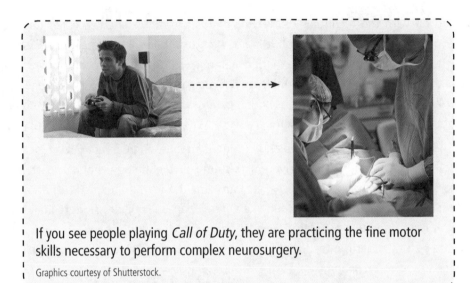

If you see people playing *Call of Duty*, they are practicing the fine motor skills necessary to perform complex neurosurgery.

Graphics courtesy of Shutterstock.

The real question is: Why are we not leveraging these types of environments for targeted learning goals?

Game designers know more about cognitive science and motivation theory than most learning professionals. Think about it. They have to design experiences that are not so hard that players get frustrated, and not so easy that players get bored. They have to create enough curiosity, appeal, or emotional connection in the game so that players will want to play the game over and over, improving incrementally as they play, for hours and hours until the player has mastered the skills required to beat the game. They have to appeal to a large—preferably diverse—audience. These games need to be so appealing that people will pay to play them in their free time, choosing to play a game over any other activity.

Have you ever seen classroom training or an e-learning course that was so well-designed people would pay to take it in their free time for fun? I'm guessing most of you would say no. If you said yes, what was it about the course that made it engaging and meaningful?

WHAT CAN ORGANIZATIONS LEARN FROM GAMES?

Organizations are starting to learn from the entertainment industry. Learning should be meaningful, but it also can—and should—be fun. People who are more engaged in their learning experiences are more likely to stick with them. People who forge an emotional connection to characters and decisions in a story line are more likely to remember them. Plus, people learn from their mistakes (University of Exeter, 2007).

Organizations have a constant need for employees, students, or members to continue to learn and develop new skills to stay competitive in an ever-changing marketplace. Providing employees with the training they need on the job can be difficult. It is often challenging to find time for employees to attend training sessions. Either training opportunities are off site and the travel time cuts into the work the employee needs to do, or the company schedules training sessions on site but the employee can't make time to attend them. Companies are becoming more global, and as a result, the training expertise within the company may not be located at the same place as the employees to be trained. Even in the case where a company may have a single office, alternate work schedules and arrangements can make on-site training sessions a challenge. In these cases, the training sessions may have to take place remotely, which can lose personal interaction.

Even if an employee can make time to attend on-site training, the training environment may not be ideal for learning. Most likely it will take place in a conference room where the trainer will stand in front of the room and lecture. There is no opportunity for the employee to see real-world examples, or to feel he is in a learning environment that would mimic his real-world environment or experiences for which he needs to be trained. In the end, companies spend lots of time and money to train employees, but not to provide them realistic contexts where they can practice applying their knowledge or receive performance feedback from experts and mentors.

BENEFITS OF IMMERSIVE LEARNING

Immersive learning offers an alternative to overcome these limitations. Not only is the organization providing better training, they are doing so at a much lower cost and higher scalability than apprenticeships, preceptorships, or other live experiential training methodologies. There are no travel costs. There are no expenses trying to develop a live simulation in real-world environments. All costs are associated with the design process and the technology platform selected to develop and deliver the learning experience, which when calculated as a per-learner cost, can become negligible depending on the size of the population that will utilize the immersive learning experience in the organization.

Learners can be located anywhere and have access to an immersive learning environment, which frees up the significant restriction geography imposes on real-world training and performance feedback from mentors and experts. Depending on the structure of your design, learning experiences can be asynchronous, allowing for learners, mentors, and experts to participate when it's convenient to them. Synchronous learning experiences provide the opportunity to give real-time feedback to a learner during or immediately following training. In some immersive environments, like virtual worlds, synchronous learning experiences can be recorded as movies, also called *machinima*. Machinima can then be utilized as training resources to leverage for later reflection and debrief of the recorded event.

As an example, in sales training, it would be possible to provide immediate feedback to an employee, as that employee is engaged in the sales process within an immersive learning environment. In real life, if a salesperson visited a customer with a more senior employee to observe the sales interaction, the salesperson would not receive corrective feedback until the sales call was over. In the best case, the observer would step in and try to rectify things with the customers and then provide feedback after the sales call was completed. In an immersive environment, it would be possible to provide the salesperson with immediate feedback at the time she did something positive or negative. In this way she could immediately identify what she did well and what she needs to improve. The possibility for the employee to receive immediate feedback within an immersive environment opens completely new opportunities to improve the overall learning process.

While a sales training exercise may seem fairly straightforward, immersive learning is relevant for any type or level of employee. A Stanford Virtual Human Interaction lab study found that physicians practicing delicate surgical procedures in virtual environments learned the procedures just as well, if not better, than their counterparts who practiced on cadavers. For learning and training, these results show that practicing desired skills in an immersive environment can be just as effective as the more expensive alternatives of preceptorships, apprenticeships, and real-world practice (Larsen, 2009). It shows that this type of learning can be applicable even for some of the most difficult real-world skills training.

Numerous studies in different contexts show the same results: Virtual practice is as effective—or more so—as real-life practice (DeAngelis, 2012). Why is this? Immediacy of feedback—corrective feedback at the time of error—plus the ability to control the training environments to ensure the most common or most difficult scenarios are experienced and navigated by learners. In real life, you learn from the experiences with which you are presented. In immersive learning, you can control what experiences learners have, the feedback they receive, and the opportunities they have to see both short-term and long-term consequences. Author Malcolm Gladwell proposes that to become an expert, you need to spend 10,000 hours in the field of desired expertise (2011). He didn't say that some of the experience couldn't be virtual. What if, through controlled immersive practice, you could reduce the amount of time it takes to achieve expertise? What would that mean to your organization, to build expertise in employees faster?

Imagine the potential for business training when employees can be trained from any location, with no risk to the company, in an environment that mimics the real world to immerse employees in the learning process, for much less cost than real-world training. Expertise can be drawn from any geographical location, at nearly any time or even on demand, and with immediate feedback for the employees so they can get real-time positive or negative responses to their actions. Obviously this has a tremendous upside over nearly any other training option that exists today. This is the power of immersive learning.

Game-based learning has been on "emerging trends" lists for years. Each year, the prediction is that organizations will finally figure out that games and immersive learning experiences are more engaging and effective than traditional classroom and e-learning courses they've delivered. Another year passes, and organizations continue to deliver didactic lectures and formulaic, templated e-learning modules...and games are on the next year's emerging trends list again.

LEARNING IN THE FUTURE

The learning industry is enormous and slow to adapt. TrainingIndustry.com estimates that the global market for training services grew to $292 billion in 2012, of which U.S. companies represent an estimated $132 billion, or 45 percent (2013). That's just organizational learning, not including K-12 education or higher education. Anywhere that people are learning, we have an opportunity to design their learning experience. Too often, those responsible for curriculum development rely on traditional didactic methodologies, even when we know that the best way to learn something is through trial and error.

Why is it so hard for organizations to adopt a new curriculum strategy that is better than their current strategy? The truth is that instructional designers, teachers, professors—the professionals who are responsible for designing and developing learning experiences—are not trained in immersive learning design. It's not because organizations don't want better learning experiences; it's because they don't have the skill or experience to design them.

In an era when rapid development tools have ruled the market, instructors assume the problem is *what* people don't know and the solution is to give them content. Immersive learning forces designers to start their process by identifying the problem, its causes, and context, instead of assuming that if you present learners with content, it will change their behavior. Sometimes the problem is *what* people don't know, but more often, the problem is *what people don't know how to do*. The problem can also be *what people are not incentivised to do*.

As learning designers, we have to be armed with the right tools to address the problem at hand. Is it a knowledge problem? If so, a rapidly developed e-learning module might do the trick. But for complex decision making or context-driven performance issues, you need to create a learning environment that allows learners to practice, fail, and learn. You need immersive learning.

THINK BIG

Here is a starting point for how to design immersive experiences: Think about how to create opportunities for practice and skill-building. Technology will change, but good design is a constant. This book provides a framework for thinking in terms of immersive learning design, outlines the process of designing for immersion, and shows real examples of how organizations have applied these principles to solve various learning and performance challenges.

As you read this book, think big. Stop thinking in terms of what people need to know, and instead think about what they need to do. Think without limitations: How would you create a learning experience that provides opportunities to practice and build expertise? Then think about the technology available to make those opportunities scalable.

There is tremendous opportunity and potential with immersive learning, but you must, in the words of Steve Jobs—think different.

SECTION 1
IMMERSIVE LEARNING

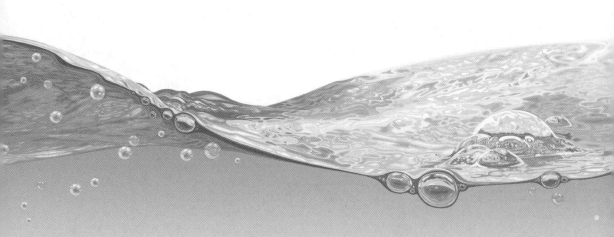

1.
WHAT IS IMMERSIVE LEARNING?

EVOLUTION OF TECHNOLOGY IN LEARNING

Before there were books, people learned by watching and practicing—trial and error. There were apprentices and squires, and knowledge was passed down through mentoring, live instruction, and feedback. This model was not scalable for many specialized skills, and the ability to learn new information, skills, or trades was limited by who you knew and who would agree to teach you. Books—as a learning technology—made instruction, if not experience, scalable. They didn't replace the previous models of instruction, but added ways to learn for those who had access to books and were literate in this new technology. Classrooms added another method of scalability: alternately leveraging lecture, discussion, reading, demonstration, and sometimes practice, to help people learn en masse.

Unfortunately, the more scalable our educational models become, the less personalized they are and the less feedback learners receive on their performance. Education becomes more about what you know and less about what you can do. Even today, our educational system and our views on how people learn are primarily shaped by delivery methods that were designed for a society with barriers. That particular society no longer exists. We have struggled to adapt our educational models as our culture and our technologies have evolved.

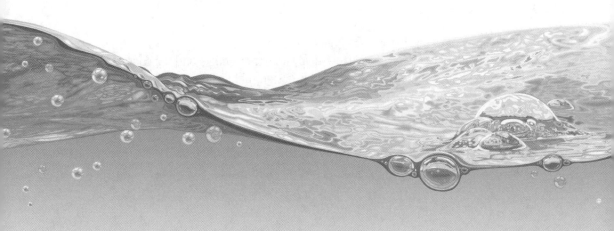

MASTER AND APPRENTICE

Knowledge was passed down through live instruction and feedback.

Graphic courtesy of Shutterstock.

TEACHER AND STUDENTS

Knowledge was passed down through a more scalable model with the introduction of the classroom.

Graphic courtesy of Shutterstock.

E-LEARNING EXAMPLE

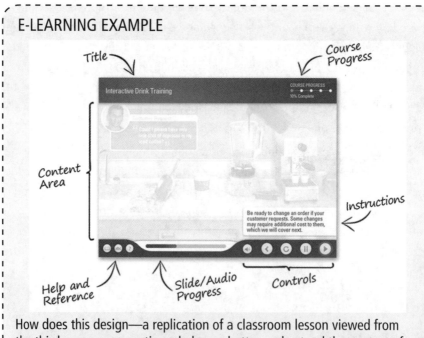

How does this design—a replication of a classroom lesson viewed from the third-person perspective—help you better understand the context of the issue? There is too much in this design that has nothing to do with what you want people to be able to do after training.

Graphic courtesy of David Charney from IllumenGroup.

In the 1990s, e-learning—or using computers as a means of delivering instruction—changed the face of adult learning. E-learning emerged as the potential of technology to provide new pathways for learning. Computers held enormous potential for delivering instruction and providing information to learners who, for any number of reasons, could not receive live classroom training and for whom books couldn't provide the necessary guidance and instruction. Organizations immediately saw the cost savings; live instruction is expensive. As e-learning became more accepted, trends emerged. Today, when people hear the term "e-learning," they typically think of a screen-by-screen page-turner module, advanced by the learner via a "Next" button, each page including text and graphics and very likely a voice-over narration, with a multiple-choice "knowledge check" every few screens and a longer multiple-choice assessment at the end.

This is not immersive learning.

While technology has continued to advance, providing new ways of interacting with information and people, e-learning design has stagnated in many ways. Instructional design degree programs primarily focus on adult learning theory, basic elements of instructional design, and models for learning experiences informed by how adults learn but that reinforce the stereotypical e-learning module format:

Repeat (Information Presentation + Reinforcement) then Assess.

There have been trends to standardize and speed up the design and development process, coined "rapid e-learning," and attempts to make this standard format more interactive than it actually is by adding attention-grabbing graphics, sounds, and more things to click on, a strategy Cammy Bean deemed "Clicky Clicky Bling Bling" (2011). But whether faster to develop or flashier to look at, most products of instructional design still adhere to the standard e-learning format established in the 1990s and replicated with wanton abandon today.

Curriculum design in education is not much better. The world is full of new technologies that allow us to interact with people and content in various ways, but classrooms today still look eerily like classrooms in the 1800s. In your average classroom, teachers are fortunate if they have access to interactive whiteboards, and students are fortunate if the teachers know how to use them as part of classroom instruction. In a 2012 survey of U.S. K-8 teachers, about half of the 505 teachers surveyed said they used games in the classroom (Barseghian, 2012). Games are not seen as core design strategies; they are still seen, even with kids, as supplemental to "real" learning activities. Although exceptions exist—like Katie Salen's school "Quest to Learn" in New York that has integrated game-based learning across its junior high curriculum (2013)—the majority of public schools have not embraced gaming or immersive learning as common instructional practice.

There are exceptions in corporate learning, too, of course. More and more organizations are looking at games as a mechanism of increasing learner engagement. Virtual worlds, particularly in some sectors, have been increasing in popularity as a technology that can change how people communicate, collaborate, and learn. Social media technologies provide tools to easily facilitate informal learning that already takes place in organizations. Mobile technology is enabling on-demand access to performance-support resources. Augmented reality is providing new opportunities to weave together games, storytelling, and real-time information access. Simulations are providing realistic environments for skill practice to organizations that invest in them.

All of these technologies and design strategies shape the way we communicate, interact, and learn, and new technologies will emerge to provide new opportunities and to address unmet needs. But unless—and until—our design practices keep up with technological advancements, we'll continue to see classroom PowerPoint presentations in virtual worlds or "game show" games created and delivered in the name of increased learner engagement. We need to move away from thinking about e-learning design in terms of reading a book or how we design classroom instruction. With the current technologies available, we're able to now recreate the apprenticeship model of instruction.

DESIGN PRACTICE WITH NO BARRIERS

The concept of immersive learning design starts with a simple question:

How would you teach someone something really important if you had no barriers?

The question is simple, but the answer (or at least, getting to the answer) is not. Let's take an example:

How would you teach someone CPR?

- Would you have them read the steps and then assess them based on whether they could remember the steps in order? Would that be enough?

- Would you have them go through a traditional e-learning module watching the steps to take, perhaps presenting different scenarios—then see if they can remember the correct steps to take given different circumstances and contexts?

- Would you have them sit in a class and have a CPR-certified instructor show them how to perform CPR on a dummy? Would you have students practice on each other?

READING ABOUT CPR

Is reading about CPR
good enough?

Graphic courtesy of Shutterstock.

...THEN TAKING A TEST ABOUT CPR

Is taking a test about CPR
good enough?

Graphic courtesy of Shutterstock.

E-LEARNING EXAMPLE

Is e-learning about CPR
good enough?

Graphic courtesy of Shutterstock.

WATCHING THE INSTRUCTOR PRACTICE CPR

Is watching CPR being performed
on a dummy good enough?

Graphic courtesy of Shutterstock.

- How much practice would you require to CPR certify someone?
- How would you measure their performance?

OK. **Now, how would you teach someone CPR if you knew that someday that person would have to use CPR correctly to save your life?**

Would you want them to simply read, listen, or watch? Or would you want them to have practiced all kinds of different techniques, with immediate feedback, on different types of patients? How much practice would you want that person to have?

CPR is a meaningful example because the skill of the person performing it could mean the difference between life and death. When someone knows what to do and how to do it, they also need to be able to do it correctly. It's also an example of a skill that is tough to really practice—and get enough practice in to be useful. Fortunately, there are not daily opportunities for everyone to practice CPR on real patients.

CHARACTERISTICS OF IMMERSIVE LEARNING

I often get the question "What's the difference between a game, a simulation, and a virtual world?" Some, like Clark Aldrich, have attempted to answer that question through discussion of features unique to each design category (2013).

Immersive learning environments actually encompass all of these mediums, and more: mobile learning, augmented reality, alternate reality games, 3-D environments, and maybe holograms someday. The truth is, the technologies and labels are blurring. Design principles of immersive learning are what bind games, simulations, and virtual worlds into this category of immersive learning environments. To a certain extent, all immersive learning incorporates each of these principles. Depending on which principle is more emphasized will lead people to label an experience a game, a simulation, or a virtual learning experience.

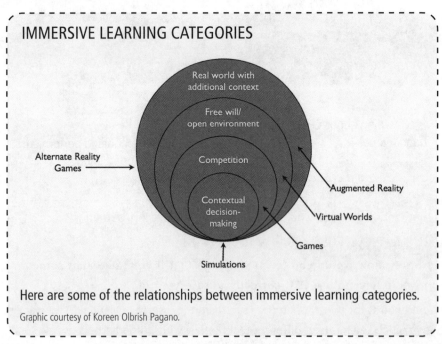

IMMERSIVE LEARNING CATEGORIES

Real world with additional context

Free will/ open environment

Alternate Reality Games ———→

Competition

Augmented Reality

Contextual decision- making

Virtual Worlds

Games

Simulations

Here are some of the relationships between immersive learning categories.

Graphic courtesy of Koreen Olbrish Pagano.

DESIGN PRINCIPLES

> **Realism:** The extent to which the environment
> in which you are immersed is lifelike.

Learning environments play a role in how effective the learning can be. Environments that have a high degree of realism may be referred to as "mirror worlds." The more realistic the environment, the easier it is for learners to make the connection between the tasks they complete in the mirror world and their real-world environment. There is a flip side to realism, however. While some tasks are easy to realistically simulate, others are much more complex or are specific to an organization. The more realistic you create your environment, the more you may challenge the learner's suspension of disbelief, especially if any of the content or setting in the environment violates their expectations.

In 3-D animations, this violation of expectations is called the "uncanny valley," which describes the human psychological reaction to seeing a human robot or 3-D character that is almost realistic, but just unreal enough to cause a strong reaction of: "This is not a real person." In immersive environment terms, this feeling will manifest itself in reactions such as, "This is not how we do things," or "That's not how a customer would really act." When this reaction occurs, the learner may dismiss the entire learning experience as unrealistic. Depending on the performance objectives, and when contextual discrepancies have the potential to derail the learner's buy-in to the practice experience, a more unrealistic environment or story line may better serve the learner's needs. Typically, the more realistic the environment, the more the experience is like a simulation.

> **Achievement:** The mechanism by which success
> toward performance goals is measured within
> the immersive learning environment.

For this design principle, you must have identified goals, a mechanism for learners to practice the skills needed to achieve these goals, and a measurement system for showing learners how close they are to achieving each goal. Think of achievement as performance metrics—or in gaming terms: how close you are to winning.

Achievement may be indicated for a single goal, or there may be multiple achievements to obtain as part of the immersive learning experience. In addition, there may be incremental achievements that help learners benchmark their progress.

Competition may be part of the achievement. One critical consideration for measuring achievement is deciding if you will benchmark against your past performance, standard accepted levels of success, or in comparison to others. Achievements may be individual or team-based. In mirror-world environments, achievements are often (and should be) the same success metrics someone would see as part of their job. For less realistic contexts, an additional "achievement layer" may be added to help learners gauge their progress against performance expectations. These achievements may take the form of high scores, badges, leveling up within the environment, or other means of special recognition.

> **Presence:** The extent to which the learner feels like she is connected or present immediately within the immersive learning environment.

Presence, in its essence, is the psychological connection that the learner makes with the tasks being performed or with the decisions being made in the immersive learning environment. One element of presence is the role of the learner within the story line. Another aspect, particularly for environments that are visually immersive, such as virtual worlds or 3-D environments, is the point of view of the learner within the environment. This point of view is either first-person or third-person. In some environments, the learner may be represented by an avatar; in some story lines, the learner is the lead character in the story. The importance of presence relates to relevant practice; if the learner feels a strong sense of presence within the environment, the practice itself will feel more real and will be more tied to performance outside of the immersive learning environment.

A FEW THOUGHTS ON IMMERSIVE LEARNING TECHNOLOGIES

This is not a book that focuses on how to build immersive learning environments, only how to design them. Yet immersive learning design assumes technology has advanced to a level that allows us to build immersive learning experiences in many ways, using different technologies. In chapter 5, much more will be discussed about the pros and cons of different technology selections for developing your immersive learning environment. For now, and to frame the design discussion in the next several chapters, here are some of the commonly used technologies that can be leveraged in immersive learning design:

- game engines
- 3-D immersive environments
- virtual worlds
- mobile technologies
- augmented reality applications
- social media platforms
- websites and basic web development tools (for example: Flash, HTML5)
- console games.

And there are sure to be new categories to add. The point is that immersive learning is not about the technology; it is about the design principles that allow learners to practice in context, apply their knowledge, and improve their skills and competence. While technology selection is an important element, there are multiple technologies that can be leveraged to create an immersive experience. The most critical aspects of immersive design are the elements that create the feeling of immersion and make the practice authentic. Technology selection should support those goals, and should not be the first step in the design process.

- - - - - - → **IT'S NOT ABOUT TECHNOLOGY, BUT ABOUT DESIGN PRINCIPLES IN CONTEXT. SEE ELMWOOD PARK CASE STUDY ON PAGE 101.**

2.
WHY SHOULD YOU USE IMMERSIVE DESIGN?

A s a design strategy, immersive learning provides a pathway to behavior change and skill improvement through features designed to emulate real performance environments. Think about the CPR example in the previous chapter. In traditional training, information is presented and (hopefully) the learner is challenged to apply that information against a few assessment questions. With immersive learning environments, you can simulate different types of emergencies, patient characteristics, and complicated issues that can allow lots of people to practice decision making combined with their CPR skills. If it was your life on the line, wouldn't you rather have someone who'd practiced with numerous virtual patients than someone who'd learned how to do CPR through an e-learning module with one or two reinforcement questions?

Most of the things people need to learn are, thankfully, not life or death. But all things being equal, when spending time, money, and other resources to help people learn, curriculum should be designed to have the maximum impact on behavior. Educators, learning professionals. and instructional designers need to constantly expand their knowledge and improve their skills to leverage the latest innovations and provide the highest learning and performance outcomes.

Physicians are expected to continually evolve their treatment of patients to include the latest medical innovations and technologies. They are required to complete continuing medical education credits each year to show this commitment to

improvement. Lawyers must complete continuing legal education credits to show their up-to-date understanding of the law. Teachers must complete continuing education courses to maintain their certification. While there is no mandatory certifying board in the learning profession, instructional designers must also evolve their professional expertise to be regarded as critical components to the success of their organizations. For curriculum designers and learning professionals, our design expertise is our specialization. Outdated design practices not only jeopardize our professional reputation, but also put our organizations at risk of losing competitive advantage in attracting the best talent and keeping employees ahead of the curve.

It is a limitation of our design that we settle for knowledge exposure when modern technology allows us to design for synthesis, skill application, and realistic practice.

ADDRESS ALL LEARNING MODALITIES

Immersive learning design is more comprehensive: It is the design of practice for behavior change and performance improvement, not just knowledge acquisition. If you consider Bloom's taxonomy, there are three domains of learning objectives that, when combined, create a comprehensive approach to learning: cognitive, affective, and psychomotor. The majority of developed curricula fall within the cognitive domain, ignoring for the most part the affective and psychomotor domains of learning. For someone to truly learn and internalize a behavior, she needs to know what to do; have an emotional connection to her performance; and have the physical skills and capability to complete the activity.

Immersive learning provides an opportunity for design to address cognition, emotion, and psychomotor skills simultaneously and in context, just as the three domains work together in the real world. This authentic practice makes learners apply what they know, while simultaneously processing how they feel about what they are doing, and building memory of the actions required to perform. For example, pharmaceutical sales representatives are constantly trained on new product information and effective selling skills that adhere to regulatory standards. Having worked in sales training for more than a decade, I've seen it is common to find sales reps who have deep product understanding (based on assessments), but who can't apply that knowledge effectively in sales conversations with healthcare professionals. It's also typical to see representatives with great salesmanship struggle when asked detailed clinical questions, and watch them lose credibility with their customers. Only by practicing sales calls in context—where they are required to synthesize and verbalize product knowledge and sales skills—can sales representatives be immersed in situations that reflect their actual performance environment. They can then truly practice the combined skills they need to execute simultaneously: clinical knowledge, product knowledge, knowledge of their customers' needs and challenges, knowledge of patients' needs and challenges, sales techniques, and relationship building, just to name a few. Immersive learning design is the only type of learning environment that demands skills be applied in context, not demonstrated in isolation. It is through this simultaneous skill application and practice that sales representatives experience what it's like to say the right words at the right time, pick up on customer cues, adjust strategy, and execute a successful sales call. These sales representatives gain the full benefit of Bloom's Taxonomy; they apply what they know, they practice what to do, and they learn how it feels. In other words, immersive design provides an opportunity for learners to gain experience.

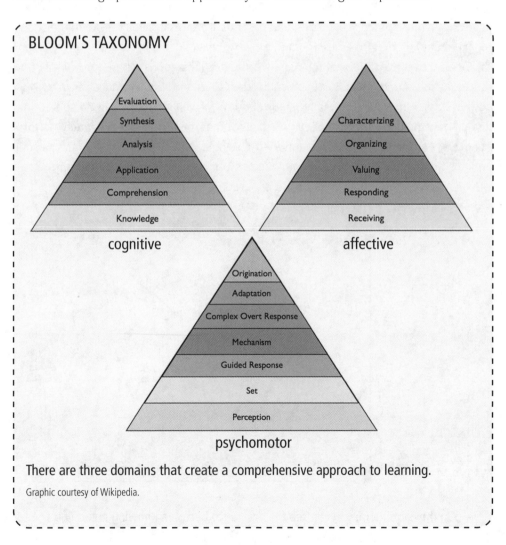

BLOOM'S TAXONOMY

cognitive

Evaluation
Synthesis
Analysis
Application
Comprehension
Knowledge

affective

Characterizing
Organizing
Valuing
Responding
Receiving

psychomotor

Origination
Adaptation
Complex Overt Response
Mechanism
Guided Response
Set
Perception

There are three domains that create a comprehensive approach to learning.

Graphic courtesy of Wikipedia.

KNOWING DOES NOT EQUAL DOING

In *The Knowing-Doing Gap*, authors Pfeffer and Sutton discuss the chasm in business between people or organizations knowing what to do and actually doing it (2000). Although there are many factors that can influence "doing," for the purposes of this book, we'll focus on instances when the issue is related to training and not to other organizational obstacles. When the barrier to behavior change is a lack of experience doing things correctly in context, immersive learning provides an opportunity to bridge the knowing-doing gap.

Learning design for doing is much different than designing for knowing. In the continuum of knowledge acquisition to behavior change, the majority of learning experiences focus on the left-most portion of the continuum—content presentation, knowledge check, recall practice activities, and perhaps scenario-based application questions, repeated until there is an assessment to prove knowledge acquisition. This cycle is typical for e-learning, and typical for most learning organizations where knowing is how success is measured, including most subjects in K–12 and higher education. Yet, what do these assessment scores really tell us about how well someone can do something? If you know the periodic table of elements, does that mean you can accurately perform science experiments? If you can identify the right way to answer a customer question on a test, does that mean you'll be able to answer that question in context on the job?

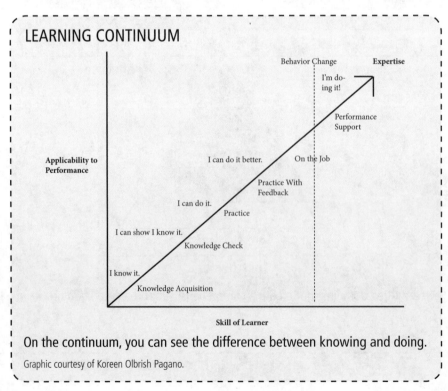

LEARNING CONTINUUM

On the continuum, you can see the difference between knowing and doing.

Graphic courtesy of Koreen Olbrish Pagano.

Once someone has proven what they know, the next step is for them to practice applying their knowledge in context. The right side of the continuum focuses on learning by doing, which is applied practice with feedback in context that allows learners to hone their skills and performance in authentic environments. This is apprenticeship, on-the-job training with coaching, internship. This is sometimes just jumping in and doing the job, learning from your mistakes along the way.

REALISTIC PRACTICE

This is also the area of the continuum where immersive learning experiences fall: where simulation, games, and virtual learning environments can provide learners with realistic practice. This allows them to learn through application but without the real risks of learning in context: loss of sales, customers, reputation, and sometimes even life. Immersive learning environments provide safe, guided practice of performance in context where learners can hone their skills and decision making without the real-world consequences of failure.

This is not to say that failure isn't an option; in truth, failure is a critical element of immersive learning environments. Without an option for failure, learners don't see what the consequences of their mistakes are. Have you ever made a big mistake, suffered the consequences, and said, "I'll never make that mistake again"? This is the opportunity that immersive learning provides: failing with safe consequences.

- - - - - → **FOR APPLIED PRACTICE WITHOUT RISKS OF REAL-WORLD FAILURE, SEE I-95 COALITION CASE STUDY ON PAGE 133.**

FEEDBACK

In addition to failure, immersive learning environments provide much more feedback than typical e-learning experiences. Think about e-learning you usually see. According to Julie Dirksen, the average e-learning module provides feedback to the learner every 5-10 minutes. Comparatively, in the average video game, players are given performance feedback every 7-10 seconds (2010). That's because games immerse you in context and everything you do provides feedback. This can actually be better than performing tasks in the real world, when you often don't see if you're successful until a task is completed; in immersive learning environments, feedback can be provided as soon as a learner makes an initial mistake, allowing opportunities for correction early in the process. For example, one study showed that surgeons who were trained by using virtual surgeries had better patient outcomes in the real world than surgeons who had trained on real patients or cadavers. Because the virtually trained surgeons were given more immediate corrective feedback on their performance, they were able to improve their skills more effectively. Also, because they were trained with "controlled" virtual patients, they were provided with more varied patient scenarios than the traditionally trained students, whose learning experiences were dependent on what types of patients they saw.

Immersive learning focuses on performance goals, not learning goals. It's the difference between being able to explain what you need to do to perform the yoga pose "downward dog" and being able to move into downward dog during a yoga workout, or between reading the music to "Twinkle, Twinkle Little Star" and playing it on a piano. The difference between knowing and doing boils down to practice to improve performance, and that is the opportunity immersive learning affords.

READING MUSIC

Reading = knowing.

Graphic courtesy of Shutterstock.

PLAYING MUSIC

Playing = doing.

Graphics courtesy of Shutterstock.

In order for immersive learning to be effective, it must allow learners chances for authentic practice. Authentic practice means the learners must complete realistic tasks or challenges, and the learner's performance must be met with realistic consequences. For example, if performance objectives for a simulation call for project managers to deliver a project on time, on budget, and without losing team members to discontent, then if any one of those parameters are not met, the learning experience should show the project, team, and personal impacts. Authentic practice environments create opportunities for learners to apply their prior knowledge (such as, "I've seen this situation happen before!"), challenge their skills in realistic settings, and see both predictable and unpredictable consequences for their actions and decisions. Authentic practice with real consequences can help to better bridge the distance between knowledge and performance. Learners are able to practice applying their knowledge and skills until they are more adept at higher level skills, more difficult tasks, and more complex decision making, with the goal of higher transfer from the learning environment to real-world application.

- - - - - - → **TECHNOLOGY CAN SIMULATE COMPLICATED SITUATIONS AND ISSUES FOR COMBINED PRACTICE. SEE MVP CASE STUDY ON PAGE 150.**

SECTION 2
THE IMMERSIVE LEARNING DESIGN PROCESS

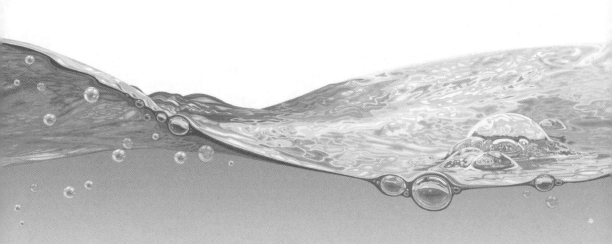

3.
ANALYSIS: IDENTIFY THE PROBLEM

GOOD OLD ADDIE AND THE IMMERSIVE LEARNING DESIGN PROCESS

ADDIE is a process model acronym that many instructional designers can recite in their sleep: a basic process model that outlines steps instructional designers should follow to create training. The steps are

- analyze
- design
- develop
- implement
- evaluate.

Let's start with disclaimers about ADDIE. ADDIE defines steps in a process, a model for stages of creating curriculum or training materials. It doesn't actually dictate the activities that happen at each stage, just what those stages are. In that way, ADDIE is both useful and flexible, but it lacks guidance on what you actually *do* in each category. ADDIE doesn't give direction for the quality of the program created, either, just

the process for getting it done. It doesn't discriminate between creating a workshop, an e-learning module, an immersive learning experience, or a bicycle. In essence, ADDIE is a checklist, a categorization for activities that should happen in any project, not just an instructional design project.

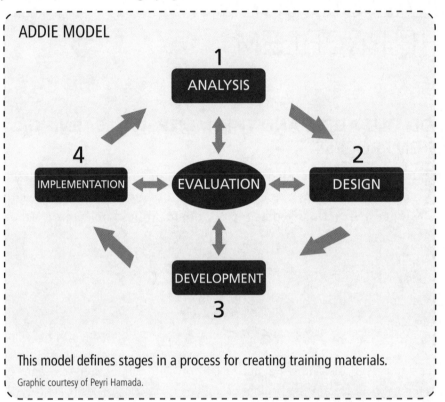

This model defines stages in a process for creating training materials.

Graphic courtesy of Peyri Hamada.

In the book *Rapid Interactive Design for E-Learning Certificate Programs* by Allen Interactions, several limitations of the ADDIE model are cited. Included in the list:

- It's not efficient because it's not iterative.
- The linear approach is effective for static content, but less so with user-generated content or open-ended content.
- It assumes you know all of the requirements before developing the content.
- It ignores the realities of project management obstacles like missed opportunities, issues with resource availability, or changing priorities.
- The process may be an obstacle to creativity (2007).

Despite its limitations, for the purposes of describing the design process for immersive learning, ADDIE serves here as an organization of activities, and guidance for the stages of the process (as well as the organization for the next four chapters). The analysis and design phases are the primary focus of this book (the AD in ADDIE), but I'll also cover basic development, implementation, and evaluation topics specific to immersive learning projects.

IDENTIFY THE PROBLEM

The most powerful tool in the immersive learning designer's tool kit is the ability to ask questions. When asked about my design process, I usually say that I spend about 80 percent of my time on analysis and 20 percent on design. The truth is, for immersive design, the results of the analysis phase inform most of what you need to design and should guide every design decision you make. Unfortunately, for as much emphasis as we put on analysis in theory, most instructional designers don't do much analysis in practice for traditional design. Typically, requirements are provided, the audience is assumed, and a solution is prescribed (such as, the VP of Sales tells you the salesforce needs an e-learning module on a new product in their portfolios).

For immersive learning design, you can't forgo the analysis, because the analysis becomes your design. Conducting a comprehensive analysis determines in large part the success or failure of the immersive learning design to provide authentic practice and help learners achieve their performance objectives. The results of the analysis help you identify what the meaningful issues are that affect performance, and create scenarios in an environment that allows learners to practice addressing those issues.

Other critical information can also be discovered during the analysis phase; issues that have nothing to do with training or practice can affect performance. One of the most common discoveries during analysis is that the compensation and rewards mechanisms within an organization are actually reinforcing behaviors you don't want to see. For example, in a recent game design workshop that I held, I challenged attendees to identify a problem within their organization they would like to solve. One of the attendees was the human resources manager at a firehouse, and the issue he wanted to solve was to get the firefighters to proactively address performance issues with each other. In just a few moments, I was able to help him figure out that the problem wasn't necessarily a training issue; it was a process issue. The conversation went something like this:

Firefighter: "What I really want them to do is be able to directly address performance issues with each other when they see someone do something wrong."

Me: "So tell me what this would look like, in an ideal scenario."

Firefighter: "Well, John would see that Joe did something wrong, and he would say something to Joe about it."

IDEAL SCENARIO

Co-workers would provide feedback to each other.

Graphic courtesy of Shutterstock.

WHAT HAPPENS NOW

Co-workers ignore the issue or go to the manager.

Graphic courtesy of Shutterstock.

Me: "What happens now if John sees Joe do something wrong?"

Firefighter: "Sometimes they say something to each other, but usually they just keep their mouths shut, or come to me with the issue, if it's serious. A lot of times, if they would say something to each other early, the problem could easily be corrected. By the time they say something to me, it's usually a major problem or something bad has happened."

Me: "Explain to me the process of what might happen if John sees Joe do something wrong."

Firefighter: "One option: John doesn't say anything, Joe continues to make the same mistake, and it becomes a big safety issue or we have a problem occur. Another option: John sees the mistake and comes to me."

Me: "Why would John come to you instead of addressing it with Joe himself?"

Firefighter: "These guys live together in the firehouse, and a lot of times they don't want to cause any issues since they are all stuck together, sometimes for days on end."

Me: "What happens if they tell you instead of telling Joe directly?"

Firefighter: "I go to Joe and address the issue to correct it."

Me: "So you fix the problem and they don't have to risk any conflict with their peers?"

Firefighter: "Yes."

Me: "Why would anyone then address issues directly with their peers?"

Firefighter: "Oh…"

I love this example, because this firefighter was so sure that the problem was a training issue since the firefighters didn't know how to directly address performance issues. He didn't see that the existing process for addressing performance issues actually discouraged firefighters from ever taking on that responsibility with each other. To be sure, the firefighters may have benefitted from immersive learning that targeted appropriate ways to address performance issues with each other to minimize conflict, but before they would start changing their behavior, the crutch of using the HR manager as the middleman needed to be removed.

FAILURE POINTS

There are myriad issues that affect performance, and many of them have less to do with what people don't know and more to do with what they aren't doing for several reasons. The reasons why people aren't doing what you want them to do, or what they know they should do, or what they want to do, lead you to "failure points." Failure points are places in performance where people don't behave in ways they should to optimize their performance. To design an immersive learning experience that allows people to authentically practice, you need to understand both where the failure points occur in the process and why they occur. Once you have identified the failure points and causes, you're prepared with the information you need to begin the immersive learning design process.

HOW TO IDENTIFY FAILURE POINTS

How do you discover the failure points and causes? While data analysis may provide you insight on where failure points occur, it's unlikely you'll find out *why* the failure points occur simply from reviewing reports. To fully define the problem that the immersive learning experience is designed to solve, there are two main methods of data collection: observation and interviewing.

OBSERVATION

Observation is by far the most direct means of collecting data on someone's performance, but it's not without challenges. While it's true that to some extent, seeing is believing, there are some limitations to observation that need to be considered. First, people's behavior changes when they know they are being observed.

It's human nature; if you know what you are supposed to do, you are more likely to do it when people are watching than when you're only accountable to yourself (Wikipedia, 2013). This isn't necessarily a bad thing; in conjunction with performance data, seeing that people know what they are supposed to do proves the problem isn't knowledge, it's something more systemic. Second, when you're observing, it's just a slice of life and may not fairly represent a typical day or typical events. Alternately, your observation period may be typical, but not reveal how people necessarily respond in unusual or extreme circumstances. To truly make observations relevant, you need to identify where and when the performance breakdown—aka failure point—occurs and observe what choices and actions people make in those situations.

GETTING THE RIGHT ANSWER

People's behavior changes when they know they are being observed.

Graphic courtesy of Shutterstock.

INTERVIEWING

In addition to—and sometimes more effective than—observation, interviewing is another way to identify failure points. Depending on the content, context, and people involved, interviewing can be done in a group setting or individually. The common goal of any kind of interview you perform is to uncover both the obvious and hidden problems and causes that will inform your immersive learning design.

The previous exchange between myself and the human resources manager/firefighter is a practical example of an interview, albeit a brief and focused one. The key to effective interviewing for immersive learning design is to get at the root of the real problem, so you can recreate it in your training environment and support learners in learning how to address the real issues that affect their performance. The danger in interviews is that you don't ask the right questions or go deep enough into the issues to be able to determine the actual failure points and causes. Think of the interview process as a series of intense, probing questions that may very well uncover some rarely discussed organizational skeletons in the closet, and you're the Barbara Walters that knows just the right questions to ask.

WHAT ARE THE RIGHT QUESTIONS?

The following questions are meant to serve as a starting point for learning how to interview effectively for immersive design, but as we've discussed throughout this book, there's no substitute for practice!

💬 What is the problem that this immersive learning solution needs to solve?

👥 Who has identified this as a problem? Who is it a problem for? Who are all of the people involved in the problem?

🙂 What would things look like if this wasn't a problem (or, what is the ideal state)?

🙁 What does it look like when this problem occurs today?

🌳 What is the environment that the problem occurs in?

❓ Why are people not performing in the way you want them to?

💧 What resources are currently available for people facing this problem?

🏅 How are people currently rewarded, recognized, or reinforced for their performance, and what are their success metrics?

 What is the problem that this immersive learning solution needs to solve?

This may seem like a straightforward question, but it's deceptively simple. The real trick to identifying the problem to be solved is that it has to be measurable. Very often, when someone is asked to define a problem, they define it in terms of nonmeasurable perceptions of desired behavior: "Sales reps need to better understand our products," or "Project managers and contracting officers need to work more collaboratively." These types of statements and descriptions reflect more of the responder's opinion than what the actual problem is, but you need to start somewhere. Through the interview process, you are not only helping the interviewees to gain better insight into the problem itself, but you are generating buy-in for how the immersive learning solution can help target the real issue and lead to behavior change.

When interviewing someone who starts out describing a problem in general, immeasurable terms that are based on opinion, focus instead on repeated, probing questions (such as the subsequent questions in this list) to get a more defined and measurable problem definition. Don't discount the opinion—remember that perception shapes reality, and your mission is to not only change behavior and improve performance, but to create a value proposition for immersive learning for both the end users and stakeholders.

Who has identified this as a problem? Who is it a problem for? Who are all of the people involved in the problem?

These are the key questions in determining who the stakeholders are and who are the people affected by the problem. In some cases, the problem directly affects the learners and they are motivated to change. In many instances, that's not the case. The problem may only be an actual problem for other members of an organization, which may or may not be motivating to learners. During this portion of the interview, focus on finding out all of the people or roles within the organization that either contribute to or are affected by the problem. Map out the relationships as part of this process to clearly understand the interconnectedness of the people and roles. Confirm those relationships with each person you interview to collect as much data as possible on how the people and relationships fit together. All of this contributes to the context of the problem to solve.

What would things look like if this wasn't a problem (or, what is the ideal state)?

Often when you're talking to someone about a problem, he can give you lots of information about everything that is wrong, but has to pause when asked what it would look like if everything was right, giving merit to the claim "everyone's a critic." Defining an ideal state is often more difficult because it illustrates how our brains try to unrealistically simplify complex environments. Working with sales representatives is a great example; often the "problem" defined is only one small aspect of what ultimately determines a sales rep's success or failure. As an example, defining the problem as, "Sales reps need more detailed product knowledge," may not actually cause a direct and measurable increase in sales if their customer relationship skills are also lacking. Reality rarely translates into easy "if, then" statements. Defining the full scope of the ideal state with measurable best practices is the only way to provide authentic practice that ultimately improves performance. In the case where sales representatives' product knowledge is defined as the problem to be addressed, the applied practice of that knowledge requires the combination of sales skills that all must be present to some degree to lead to successful sales performance.

For this portion of the interview, focus on all of the skills and attributes that constitute successful performance, not just the ones identified as the problem. Collecting data on the full scope of the performance environment is what differentiates authentic immersive learning environments from isolated skill practice. By creating a visualization of the ideal state, with the interrelationship of the people and roles defined, you will identify what success metrics and decisions are critical for performance improvement in your immersive learning design, plus those secondary issues and decisions that affect overall success.

What does it look like when this problem occurs today?

Once you have established a clear picture of the desired end state, it's time to backtrack and find out all of the ways in which the current state differs. Presumably, you have a well-defined, measurable problem and you know where you want people to end up, but you need to know how far they have to go to get there.

This portion of the interview is where you establish that baseline of current performance, identify the failure points where performance deviates from the ideal state, and establish the rationale for why those deviations are occurring. This is also, often, the most difficult information to obtain because, frankly, people love to critique but rarely feel comfortable identifying the true underlying causes for why performance isn't ideal. Especially if the rationale for failure points is institutional in nature—for example, a result of current structure, processes, procedures, or success metrics.

Performance improvement is *not* a training problem in those instances; it is an organizational change problem. There is no immersive learning experience that will improve performance in a system that doesn't reward and support ideal performance. In order for immersive learning to be an effective performance improvement tool, it must be implemented in an environment that supports and rewards the desired performance. Uncovering that the problem is not a training problem could make you pretty unpopular.

If you establish that the problem is not—or not only—a training or practice issue, but a bigger systemic organizational problem, the results of the analysis phase should prompt you to address those systems before you undertake immersive learning design. While it may seem counterintuitive for a book on the immersive learning design process to steer you away from immersive design as a solution, consider this: If the goal of immersive learning is to allow for authentic practice, and the real-life context doesn't support reinforcement of the performance goals you've established, what is the likelihood that any training solution or practice environment will be effective in achieving behavioral change? Why set your design up for failure?

The purpose of the interview process is to uncover the details of performance context so that they can be recreated in the immersive design. If the context is the problem, even the best, most authentic immersive learning environment will end up replicating your current performance issues, because the system is reinforcing them. For immersive learning to be effective, it must mirror the performance environment, and the performance environment must reinforce the desired behaviors.

Hopefully, you don't uncover system problems through the interview process and you are able to determine both the failure points and the rationale for the failure. As part of the interview, this discovery process should sound something like this:

- What happens first in the process?
- What can go wrong at this stage?
- Why might that go wrong?
- Is there any other reason it might go wrong?
- Are there any other things that could go wrong?
- Why might that happen?
- Are there any other reasons that might happen?

Truly, your goal in this phase is to uncover every little problem, every little nuance, and add it to your context map. But this time, this isn't the ideal state, this is the "everything that can go wrong and probably does" state. It is all of the problems, nuances, issues, and causes that will be woven together to create the fabric of your immersive learning environment. The process, the people, and their motivations and failures are what ultimately create the practice that allows learners to make mistakes in training, so that performance is improved in the real world. It is your responsibility to uncover those details here.

What is the environment that the problem occurs in?

If you haven't already established all of the performance contexts, this question will uncover them. As important as it is to uncover the process and steps in performance, it's also critical to understand the performance environment.

Questions to support this discovery process could include:

- Are people working on their own or in teams?
- Are people geographically dispersed or all in one location?
- Are people all working synchronously, or does work happen asynchronously?

- How is communication occurring and what technologies are used?
- What is the actual physical environment like and how does that affect the process or performance?
- What other pressures are being put on the people expected to perform these tasks?

As you're preparing your immersive learning canvas, the *where* of performance may be just as important as the what or how. Digging into where people are expected to perform will inform your design to be more visually representative, and will also help you include realistic details to connect the practice environment with the performance environment.

Why are people not performing in the way you want them to?

Maybe the current structure isn't reinforcing the behaviors you want to see, or maybe people need training or more practice to apply what they know effectively. But it's also possible there are outside influencing factors that affect performance. Take time in the interview to investigate who the people are that are being asked to change their behavior. While personality differences can play a role, other things like the hiring profile or the employee demographics—including age, gender, ethnicity, race, socio-economic status, level of education, or previous experience—could all play a role in influencing the current performance outcomes. Maybe your system is structured in a way to reward the behavior you want to see, but the reward system doesn't motivate the particular group of employees you are trying to reach. Digging deeper into the characteristics and culture of your target learners will help you better assess the effectiveness of the institutional structure and processes, but it will also help you create an immersive learning experience more relevant to your audience.

What resources are currently available for people facing this problem?

Chances are, this isn't the first time people have been trained on the problem and it's probably not the first time that someone has tried to support or improve performance. It's also likely the learners themselves have been taking action to try to improve their performance through informal learning measures with their peers or managers. These existing resources and strategies shouldn't be ignored or abandoned; they should be leveraged as part of the arsenal of tools that can be accessed in the immersive learning environment.

Take time in the interview process to find out what resources, tools, and people are currently available to support performance and investigate how employees are using those resources—or not. The most telling information may be the DIY support systems and how people augment the formal training and support structures to get information and insights they need. Asking people directly about how they currently get support will provide additional context and reality to the immersive learning experience. Talk to the high performers. Why are they doing it right? What resources do they use?

How are people currently rewarded, recognized, or reinforced for their performance, and what are their success metrics?

When organizations are aligned, their reward and recognition systems align with their performance metrics and organizational success metrics. Hypothetically, you tell people what you want them to do, you reward them for doing it well, and the organization is successful. As you complete your interview process, where you have collected information about the audience, context, environment, resources, and so on, you should also formally collect information on how performance is rewarded within the organization. This serves two purposes. First, you can determine how effective the rewards system is by looking at all of your qualitative data compared to your quantitative data on performance. Second, it will provide you a realistic scoring structure to emulate within the immersive learning environment. Ideally, the success metrics should align with your ideal state goals. If not, now would be the time to address those rewards systems to ensure that performance after the immersive learning experience is reinforced appropriately.

THINK ABOUT HOW PEOPLE ARE CURRENTLY REWARDED. SEE GOVLOOP CASE STUDY ON PAGE 105.

ANALYSIS SUMMARY

So you've collected and reviewed the quantitative data and performance reports. You've observed performance in the field and collected data through those observations, plus through interviews with key stakeholders and target learners. You've created process maps that show the relationships between people and roles, and where failure points occur and why. In short, you've clearly defined your problem and identified your end performance goals.

The work that you've done in this analysis phase is the primary foundation of your design work. While it would be great if you could do an initial analysis phase and cleanly move on to the design phase, the truth is that analysis will be ongoing and more data may present itself. Your goal should be to approach immersive design from a position of a questioner: never assuming an answer, and always seeking new sources of information to make your immersive environment as effective as possible. Only when immersive learning is aligned in this way can you achieve the ultimate goals of behavior change and performance improvement.

4.
DESIGN: CREATE THE WORLD

DESIGNING IMMERSIVE LEARNING

Maybe you're an instructional designer who realizes the potential of emerging technologies for designing learning experiences, but don't know how to get started. Or maybe you're a subject matter expert tasked with training people on what you know, in the hopes of improving their performance by passing along your expertise. Maybe you're a college professor or teacher who wants to engage students with content differently, in context, to show the application of what they are learning. Or maybe you're an executive who is no longer satisfied with training that presents content but doesn't actually give people in your organization an opportunity to practice what you want them to be able to do.

Forget everything you think you know about designing curriculum. What you need to be doing is designing *practice*. So where do you begin?

Designing immersive learning requires three levels of design decisions that work in conjunction with each other but that should also be thought of as their own separate, parallel processes.

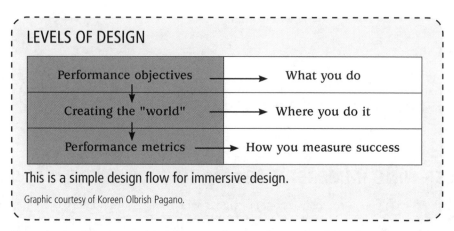

LEVELS OF DESIGN

Performance objectives ⟶	What you do
Creating the "world" ⟶	Where you do it
Performance metrics ⟶	How you measure success

This is a simple design flow for immersive design.

Graphic courtesy of Koreen Olbrish Pagano.

First, the performance objectives need to be determined. Performance objectives are different from learning objectives; performance objectives focus on what the learner should be able to do rather than know. Often in a work environment, employee performance is evaluated based on performance metrics. For salespeople, it might be number of new customers acquired, number of units sold, or a revenue target. For customer service representatives, it might be how many customer issues are resolved in a set amount of time, or it might be the average time to resolution for customer service calls. For project managers, it might be hitting project timeline and budget targets. Managers and educators alike have probably heard of SMART goals: specific, measurable, attainable, relevant, and time-bound. These are the same parameters that should guide your development of performance objectives.

Immersive learning should be designed to change behavior and improve performance. In order to do that and to measure that it's been done, you need to have initial performance benchmarks (for example, what can the person already do) and performance objectives (such as, what do you want the person to be able to do). The design of the immersive learning experience then focuses on getting learners from benchmark to goal through realistic practice.

UNDERSTAND THE PERFORMANCE ENVIRONMENT MORE DEEPLY. SEE QUE SYRAH SYRAH CASE STUDY ON PAGE 108.

The second level of design is creating the world your learners will be immersed in. This is the story, the characters, the places, and the plot. These are all of the elements in the immersive environment that need to be designed to create practice opportunities. The design of the world should be based on your performance objectives and an analysis of the audience. In the analysis phase, you collect information you need to fully define the audience and performance environment; based on that information, you can create the world to best match your objectives.

The third level of design is performance evaluation. These are the achievements and progress benchmarks that are designed to support your learners achieving their performance objectives while seamlessly integrating with the immersive learning environment. Performance metrics are one of the key elements identified in the analysis phase, and they inform design decisions of how to mark progress and evaluate learner performance.

THE "F" WORD

Yes, we were going to get to it eventually. The "F" word: fun. Or its four-letter counterpart: play. Even a few short years ago, I couldn't walk into a company and talk to them openly about designing games for learning. The concepts of fun and play were seen as distracting from learning; they didn't exemplify the seriousness of what most organizations were trying to accomplish with their training programs. Learning, they thought, was serious business.

That's not to say that companies didn't use games for learning. Many organizations actually did incorporate games, but you couldn't call them that. I typically referred to them as "competitive learning environments." I even worked with one pharmaceutical company who wouldn't use the term "role play"—we had to call them simulated sales calls or realistic practice activities.

Luckily, times have changed. With the emergence of social games, mobile app games, and the much-debated term "gamification," many organizations now recognize the value of games and game mechanics used for learning. Humans like to play. We like to learn. We like to learn by playing. Even when (or especially when) the subject matter is extremely serious, adding elements of playfulness into learning can keep our interest and can encourage repetitive practice and exposure to important content. When was the last time you went through an e-learning module more than once? Then think: How many games do you only play one time?

The problem with fun is that it is subjective; the problem with play is that it is defined, in part, as fun. If you ask 10 people their favorite game, you will more likely than not get 10 different answers. If you ask why that game is their favorite, they will provide you answers that help you understand what they define as fun: socializing with friends, solving challenging puzzles, physical exercise, or sometimes just winning or feeling skilled at a game makes the experience of play "fun" (Koster, 2004).

The value of games for learning is not just for players to have fun; it is the very way they are designed that encourages people to play again and again and again. Games encourage practice and are designed to assume it takes the player many tries to get skilled enough to win the game. It is not assumed that a player will always be able to win a game. While some games allow players to hone skills to advance, others add elements of risk and chance that can help players succeed or can challenge them to overcome obstacles. Both of these design constructs encourage replay ability: You get progressively better at the skills necessary to win the game, or you get better at figuring out how to overcome any obstacles that impede your success. Either way, the game remains a challenge, which is an essential element of designing an experience that is fun.

THE OTHER "F" WORD

There is a name for the feeling that immersive learning aspires to create in learners: flow. Flow theory was proposed by Mihaly Csíkszentmihályi as a term to describe:

> "The mental state of operation in which a person in an activity is fully immersed in a feeling of energized focus, full involvement, and success in the process of the activity. According to Csíkszentmihályi, flow is completely focused motivation. It is a single-minded immersion and represents perhaps the ultimate in harnessing the emotions in the service of performing and learning. In flow, the emotions are not just contained and channeled, but are positive, energized, and aligned with the task at hand" (Wikipedia, 2013).

As immersive learning designers, the goal state of our designs should be flow, where learners are connected to the content and actively involved with the tasks they are presented. Whether it is a game, simulation, story-line driven learning experience, or 3-D virtual environment, the design of the experience should be such that learners are actively involved and invested in the outcome of the experience.

The figure on the next page shows the range of emotional response occurring in learners when skill and challenge levels aren't evenly matched. These emotional responses represent the mental state and the engagement level of learners presented with learning experiences across the spectrums of their skill level and the activity's challenge level. So how does this relate to immersive learning design?

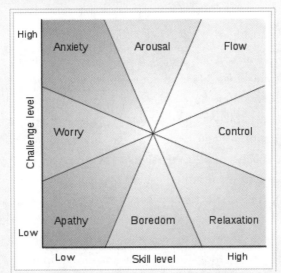

THE EMOTIONAL RESPONSES OF FLOW

With different challenge and skill levels, there are varied emotional responses.

Graphic courtesy of Wikipedia.

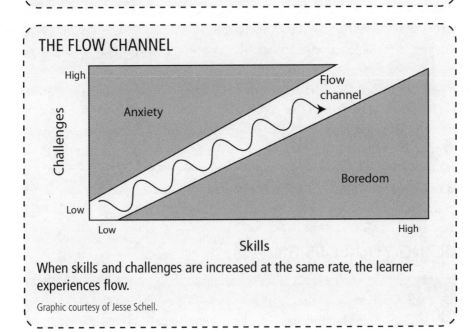

THE FLOW CHANNEL

When skills and challenges are increased at the same rate, the learner experiences flow.

Graphic courtesy of Jesse Schell.

The explanation is simple, but the actual execution is very, very difficult. To keep learners in the flow channel, you need to increase the difficulty level of the activities at the same rate that the learner's skill increases to keep the learner from getting anxious or bored (and therefore keeping her engaged in the learning experience). In his book *The Art of Game Design*, Jesse Schell uses the prior graph to demonstrate the "flow channel" designers should strive for to keep players engaged (2008).

As an immersive learning designer, you have several challenges to obtaining flow. First, you need to know what skill level your audience will start out at when engaging in the experience. Second, you have to account for variability in that skill level to keep learners of different capabilities engaged (or limit the audience range). Another consideration is the amount of content you plan on presenting to learners. In truth, this may be the biggest challenge for immersive learning design. If you think about traditional e-learning, content is presented, then knowledge checks, more content, more checks, and then maybe one or two application exercises or scenarios. Contextualized challenges are limited in number, which reduces the content development burden of the designer. For immersive learning, however, the goal is contextualized practice, so more content is necessary, both in amount and in complexity. This requires the designer to take on the responsibility to understand the performance environment at a level that is not required for most non-immersive training modules or workshops.

To reach flow in immersive learning, there must be enough experiences the learner can engage in to incrementally assess and provide feedback on his performance. Model-based simulations allow for a greater variety of learner inputs and results, but challenge the designer to prepare performance-specific feedback in advance for all of the potential performance outcomes. Completely open environments, like virtual worlds, often require an expert or coach to be present to observe the learner's performance and provide feedback. More predictable content paths allow designers to create more specific, relevant feedback for each decision or action, but they typically don't provide as much opportunity for replay or variability of experience. Although your choice of design structure will depend largely on the problem your immersive learning experience seeks to address, it is important to be aware of how each of your design decisions affect flow, and to structure your experience to maximize learner flow potential.

STARTING YOUR DESIGN

After conducting the analysis and defining the problem to be solved, it's time to start designing your immersive learning environment. Based on the data you've collected, you may already have some inclinations as to what type of immersive environment might work best for the particular audience, context, and performance goals. It is during the design phase that the connections are made between the performance goals and the story line, with the success measures supporting progress from baseline performance to goal achievement.

In the fall of 2011, I taught a "Game and Simulation Design" graduate course at Harrisburg University. As a class project, students were asked to build a design document week by week for an immersive learning environment. Because the class was focused on design, we began by simulating an abbreviated version of the analysis phase that required the students to define the problem, context, and audience for their immersive learning design, which we synthesized into an executive summary. For the remainder of the course, we systematically tackled the key elements of the design document; I'm recreating that structure here as guidance for an immersive learning design structure. One aspect of immersive learning design is that it's less linear and compartmentalized than traditional e-learning because everything is presented in context. Similarly, it's difficult to create a compartmentalized and linear design document and systematic design process, because everything is interconnected: characters, story line, environment, performance objectives, feedback, rewards, and so on. Still, design decisions and structure need to be documented to hand off from designers to developers, so creating a document that details all of the components while describing their interconnections, feedback cycles, failure responses, and success indicators is critical.

Here is a basic outline for a game design document.

GAME DESIGN OUTLINE

- Goal
- Theme & Story Line
- Instructional Strategy
  - Target Audience
  - Learning and Performance Objectives
- Play
  - Learner Role
  - Game Structure
  - Team Structure
  - Non-Player Characters
  - Clue Distribution
- Game Components
- Tracking and Scoring
  - Individual vs. Team
  - Story-Line Points
  - Bonus Points and Content
- Portal Functionality
  - Player Perspective
  - Non-Player Character Perspective
- Content
  - Scenarios
- Schedule

This is a part of the sample game design outline. To see the full sample, go to astd.org and search for "Immersive Learning."

Graphic courtesy of Koreen Olbrish Pagano.

The remainder of this chapter will describe the content to be included in each of those sections, with examples of the design decisions that need to be made through its completion.

STORY LINE

The story line is the world you are creating in which your learners will practice what you want them to be able to do. In constructing this world and the story line, there are several aspects to consider in defining the learner experience. Think about your decisions around story line as the things you'd have to decide if you were writing a book. First, are you writing a collection of short stories that have a central or connecting theme, or are you writing a novel with a longer story line that builds upon itself and develops over time? In immersive design, the "short story collection" metaphor might apply if you need learners to practice a variety of skills in isolation, then practice putting them all together. For example, if you were teaching someone to crochet, you might have them practice each of the stitches first before putting them all together to make a sweater. Similarly, if you were teaching someone to play golf, you might isolate long drives, chip shots, and putting as separate skills before playing a round of golf. Contrast that with a "novel" design strategy that might be appropriate when allowing someone to practice project management or customer service skills. The performance objectives for your immersive learning experience, and the most effective way to practice and apply them, will inform your decision for the structure of your story line.

After determining your story-line structure, the next major decisions are about tone and theme. While the terms "immersive learning" and "authentic practice" imply that the tone of your story line needs to be realistic, that is not always the case; in fact, there are some situations that a realistic story line might actually impede learning and practice instead of supporting it.

An example of this is "The Change Game," developed with Resilience Alliance as a game that allowed players—when faced with organizational change—to see characters struggle with seven personal resilience factors, and to practice identifying which character struggled with which factor. Initially, this game was designed to be rolled out to employees of a major car company at both the dealership level and the corporate offices. The company had been implementing numerous new policies in response to changing market dynamics, but were facing resistance from employees at all levels of the organization, resulting in uneven adherence to the new policies and problems for the company in reaching their organizational goals. Basically, change was not happening and much of the resistance was at the individual level.

SEE MORE ABOUT THE CHANGE GAME CASE STUDY ON PAGE 117.

They could have created an immersive learning solution—in this case, a game— that took place in a dealership and used actual, specific examples to highlight how people were resisting the changes and how that was affecting the organization. But there were some drawbacks to that approach. First, if they created scenarios at the dealership level, the scenarios wouldn't have applied to employees in the corporate offices. Even at the dealership level, it would be difficult to create scenarios that were applicable to employees across the sales, finance, and repairs departments. Besides the difficulty in making situations relevant across a varied audience, if they created scenarios that were contextualized to their actual organizational changes, the game would only be relevant for a relatively short time. The company was interested in an ongoing improvement of a higher resiliency to change across the organization. They wanted to use the game as a way to build a vocabulary of resilience with existing employees as well as with all new hires. Because of this, they needed a story line with a more universal context, so employees could relate to it without taking it personally. Finally, the company realized that if they used a realistic story line, employees might be quicker to dismiss scenarios that did not exactly mirror their work environment, and the goal of the training was to improve resiliency in general, not just in relation to specific changes. They wanted to make sure learners were focused on resilience to any change, not just to a specific change the organization was trying to implement. For all of these reasons, a realistic setting and story line would have impeded the purpose of the learning. Instead, the story line of the game put the learner as a crew member on a spaceship with a new captain who was implementing many changes, to which the crew was responding with varied levels of resilience. By applying realistic scenarios in a fantastical environment and theme, players were able to focus on characters' responses to change without being distracted by how applicable the context was to their current roles and responsibilities.

That said, in many cases, to authentically practice, a realistic context is important. Through the analysis phase, you should have uncovered the critical contextual elements that affect performance to recreate them in your design. For realistic designs, those elements build the foundation of your immersive learning environment and are the pillars of your theme. That's not to say that having a realistic theme dictates a serious tone; depending on your audience analysis, you may decide to incorporate a more humorous or whimsical tone into your realistic scenarios and environment. Each of your decisions should be informed by your analysis, with thought as to how your design choices will not only affect learner perception of the experience, but also how each choice potentially affects the performance outcomes.

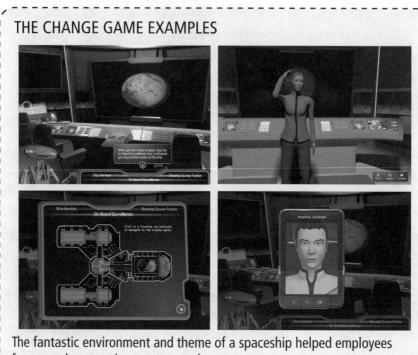

THE CHANGE GAME EXAMPLES

The fantastic environment and theme of a spaceship helped employees focus on characters' responses to change.

Graphics courtesy of Tandem Learning and Dr. Linda Hoopes.

After selecting your story-line structure, theme, and tone, there are other story-line parameters to define to further construct your environment:

- **Locations:** Where are the locations that learners are expected to perform or interact with each other? Think about including not only the performance environments, but also typical locations where learners would prepare for their performance, places where people communicate and interact as part of the process, and where learners receive feedback and coaching. Don't limit your idea of locations to physical locations; email, voicemail, corporate communication systems, smartphones, and social media sites might also be important "locations" in your story line.

- **Moment in time:** Not only do you need to determine where the story line takes place, but you also need to determine when. While most immersive learning experiences probably won't take place in the past, you may choose to set your story line in the future to provide some distance from current circumstances that might distract from the goals.

- **Timeline:** Depending on your performance goals, you'll need to determine if the passing of time within your immersive learning environment is critical to either practice or feedback. This is particularly important if the implications of actions or decisions aren't immediate; some decisions won't have positive or negative impacts for days, months, or sometimes years. In these cases, you may want to accelerate time, or jump into the future, to show learners the long-term consequences of their performance.

- **Characters:** As part of the story-line decisions, you will need to determine the cast of characters who are critical to the context of performance. In the next section, we'll focus on character development, but as part of your story-line development, you'll need to develop your cast list.

After you've decided on the basics of your world, it's time to construct the story. For most design documents, the story-line section will outline the introduction to the story, the major plot and decision points (that coincide with the failure points identified in the analysis phase), and the decision options for each. You might think of this as a content outline, but it's more of a "context outline," or experience map. If you collected the appropriate contextual data during the analysis phase, the story line will likely be a series of scenarios and decision points. These scenarios will present learners with opportunities to fail as they collect feedback and experiences that move them along the continuum of current to desired performance levels.

CHARACTERS IN DETAIL

It may be the case that your particular immersive learning environment doesn't have any people in the story except the learner; this is sometimes the case for simulations, and especially equipment simulations. In general, however, people's performance environments involve and depend on other people, whether as part of a team, or simply in a structure where they are responsible to or for others. These are the people that make up the cast of characters in your immersive learning environment, and they are important because these characters hold within them the opportunity for learners to make an emotional connection, either in a positive or negative way.

If you think about your favorite characters, whether in movies, television shows, or books, the common thread is that you care what happens to them. Even the villains—you want to see them defeated or you begin rooting for them, either because you identify with their complexity or you hope for their redemption. It is our ability to connect with characters in stories that creates an emotional connection. You feel like you know them.

While immersive learning environments may not have the same character development potential as entertainment media, that doesn't mean character development should be ignored. One of the best ways to engage and motivate learners is for them to feel an emotional connection or responsibility to the characters in your story line. To establish that connection, think about how to develop characters that have personality characteristics and backstories that learners can identify with. Create opportunities for learners to develop relationships with the other characters beyond simple task completion.

VILLAIN!

You know who he is...

Graphic courtesy of Shutterstock.

Our day-to-day interactions with other people are full of emotion that affects the way we talk to each other, affects our decisions and actions, and places value on how what we do affects others. Our relationships with and knowledge of other people on a personal level affect our decisions, often unconsciously: Are you more understanding of an employee who's late because you know she has a sick child at home? Are you more nervous talking to certain supervisors because they tend to fly off the handle at the smallest issues? These are the types of things that affect real performance, but won't show up on an analytics report. In an immersive learning environment, learners have the chance to see how these interpersonal dynamics affect their performance, and the chance to practice approaching people and situations more effectively.

For each character in your immersive learning environment, define the character's role in relation to the learner. For example, one of your characters might be Nina Sommerfleck, a writer on your project team, or Sam Taylor, your manager who provides coaching and advice on your performance. Some characters might play minor roles, or only show up for one or two scenarios, while others—your major characters—may be involved in your story line throughout. How important each character is to your story line, and the impact he has on performance, should dictate how much of a history and personality you develop for that character.

There are lots of character development checklists for writers that will give you ideas and parameters for how to flesh out your characters. Completing these lists for a character does not mean that all of these details will show up in your story line, or will be relevant for your immersive learning environment. Completing a character profile will simply help you write better characters, understand their motivations, and bring your story line to life in a way that typically doesn't happen with flat, uninteresting, stereotypical characters in e-learning. You can find many examples online, but as a starting point, I've included some basic "interview" questions that you might consider to support the development of your character profiles:

- What is the character's name, gender, race, age, and family background?
- How would someone stereotype this character at first glance?
- Does this person have a romantic partner or friends?
- What is this person's job and socioeconomic status?
- What makes this person happy? Sad?
- What are this person's personality characteristics and fears or phobias?
- Who is this person's nemesis?

This is just a starting point; for minor characters, you may not even require this much detail and for major characters, you may need more. Focus on the characters' motivation for their behavior, then make sure their actions, conversations, and interactions are consistent with who they are. This consistency and insight into your characters will make them easier to write into your story line and will help your learners connect with them.

ROLE OF THE LEARNER AND IMPLICATIONS OF AVATARS

You've created your story line and you've created a cast of characters. Now, what character does the learner play in this immersive learning environment? Does this representation match who they are in real life, or is it altered to show an entirely different side of them? And who do others perceive them to be?

To begin, think about perspective. How does the learner interact with the world? Is the interaction from a first-person perspective, where the learner has direct interactions and impacts on the environment, but everything is "seen" through the learner's eyes? Is the learner an omnipresent observer, not actually able to affect the visual environment, but is watching the interactions of the other characters and reflecting on these decisions and interactions? Maybe your learner has the role of master of the immersive learning universe, able to make big, omnipotent decisions and then see how those decisions affect the environment and characters. Depending on your performance goals and the analysis that is informing your design, any of these options might best suit your goal.

Perhaps the most interesting and researched role of the learner in immersive environments has been the third-person perspective, or the learner controlling a character within the story line that the learner can see within the environment. The physical representation of yourself in a virtual environment has been labeled an "avatar." An avatar is some representation of you over which you have control and through which you are able to interact (for example, communicate, move, react) in an immersive environment, such as a 3-D game or virtual world. While the avatar represents you in the world, it is not required to have any similarity to how you look, act, talk, or generally appear to others in the real world. Sometimes, an individual has the opportunity to create an avatar to look and behave however he chooses. This is one of the major attractions of immersive environments: They allow people to assume different identities and try new attitudes and behaviors, regardless of their identity in the real world.

A USER WITH A SIMILAR AVATAR

Sometimes users like to choose similar characters.

Graphic courtesy of AcidCow.com.

A USER WITH A DIFFERENT AVATAR

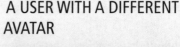

Sometimes users prefer to choose very different characters.

Graphic courtesy of Robbie Cooper.

Avatars, simply defined, are a representation of you in a virtual environment. This is an important distinction: Avatars in an immersive learning environment not only represent you, but they are you, conveying a sense of your physical presence in a digital environment. Your avatar's actions are your actions and your avatar's experiences are your experiences. Avatars can therefore perform tasks and accomplish goals for you—perhaps even better than you. For example, research done at Stanford's Human-Computer Interaction Lab found that as little as 90 seconds of chatting and interacting with an avatar is enough to cause behavioral changes in the real world (Yee and Bailenson, 2009). The implications of this are truly enormous. It means that as little as a minute and a half of conversation or interaction between two avatars can change how the real life people controlling those avatars behave. In the workplace, employees could hone their presentation skills, coaching conversations, selling skills, and more by engaging in practice activities with their avatars, achieving very significant results in very little time.

What it is about avatars that allow them to cause this type of change? One answer is a user's projection of self onto his avatar. The Stanford Virtual Human Interaction Lab found that people start to experience real-world physiological responses to the virtual world stimuli that their avatars encounter. For example, if your avatar is "bumped into" by another avatar, then you may experience a real-life physiological response, just as if someone had bumped into you. Feeling embarrassment or shyness in immersive environment situations are other examples of this. As the immersive learning environment is not real, there should be nothing within the world itself that would cause embarrassment or shyness. It is merely a computerized environment. Because users project themselves onto their avatars, feelings and emotions come into play within an immersive learning environment.

Identification of the user with her avatar is a critical step in building this type of response. Some key features of avatars can build the emotional connection between the user and the avatar. The ability to express emotion, to develop a unique appearance, and to interact with the virtual world environment and other avatars within the environment are some of these key features (Fox et al, 2012).

It should be noted that identification with an avatar is not immediate for the user. Upon first creating and using an avatar there is some period of time where the user must get comfortable with the technology itself and must learn to be able to create, modify, and utilize the avatar. Once this stage is passed, the user must then begin to feel some emotional connection to her avatar to the point where the user cares about the avatar and begins to see the avatar as herself. Beyond this threshold, users must then struggle with what role or roles an avatar will play for them and whether or not their avatars can meet those roles. All of this takes time, and the amount of time can vary from individual to individual; however, it is typically not an instant connection. For additional details on the steps in the process, Dr. Steven Warburton presented work on the development of avatar identity (Warburton, 2008).

There are some interesting parallels between how avatars are perceived and how we perceive others in real life. Just as has been shown in real-world interactions, people have more positive opinions and more interactions with avatars they define as attractive, and alternately have more negative opinions and less interactions with avatars perceived as unattractive (Nowak and Rauh, 2006 and Yee and Bailenson, 2007). For work, this has interesting implications. For example, a person who is perceived as unattractive in real life may find that his interactions and work relationships improve as a result of having an attractive avatar. Or alternatively, an attractive person who creates an unattractive avatar may find that business relationships suffer in the virtual world. Should an elderly person choose to create a younger avatar to avoid any ageism within an immersive learning environment, or should employees represent themselves accurately?

Questions about the role of the learner, and specifically when the learner is represented by an avatar in an immersive learning environment, should be answered by the data collected during the analysis phase. Is it important for the learner to practice decision making from her own perspective, or is it critical for the learner to understand the complexity of decision making from another person's point of view? Depending on the answers appropriate for you to achieve your performance goals, you may choose to allow learners to highly customize their avatars in the environment to increase their feelings of connectedness. Alternately, you may determine that personalization of avatars is unnecessary, or in some cases distracting from the learning or performance goals.

For organizations that are transitioning to immersive learning as an ongoing, pervasive design strategy, reusability and the ongoing connectedness between the learner and his avatar is a serious consideration. Avatars may be developed as part of the new hire orientation process, introducing new employees to the immersive learning environment and beginning the connection between employee and avatar. The new employee's avatar could go through "on-the-job" training in the immersive learning environment before the employee is ever asked to perform her job in real life. Training, coaching, and assessment could all happen in an immersive environment on a much more consistent basis than is typically possible in any organization, but especially in organizations with large populations of remote workers or remote offices. Depending on the technology selected to support the immersive learning, social events or meetings could be organized with little advanced notice, providing more informal learning opportunities and more options for receiving insights and feedback about successes and failures from managers, mentors, or peers.

Another potential impact for the role of the learner is the chance to walk a mile in someone else's shoes. Avatars and immersive environments open up a whole new dimension in diversity and cultural training. Since it is very easy for a black person to be white, a man to be a woman, a young person to be older, and so on, the selection of avatars within immersive environments can provide very valuable information to businesses seeking to gain a better understanding of different races, genders, and ages. Avatars allow learners to experience how it may feel to be someone other than who they are. If a business was moving into new global marketplaces, an immersive environment would offer the opportunity for employees to create avatars to represent their customers or fellow employees from other regions around the world. Through this, they could gain experience learning about these other cultures—including language, customs, history—without the expense and hassle of travel. This demonstrates the power of immersive learning, and particularly avatars and what they can represent.

At an enterprise level, avatars give employees another venue to express themselves, interact with others, learn, and grow personally and professionally. They are the cornerstones of 3-D immersive experiences, and developing strong identification between employees and their avatars helps employees engage with their virtual work environment in a way that is most beneficial to them personally as well as to the organization as a whole.

Avatars present an opportunity to level the playing field for employees who have disabilities that impair their interactions with others in real life. Deaf employees can interact with others via text chat in a much more interactive way than they may be able to in real life. Employees with physical disabilities that may prevent them from participating fully in social events or even in attending meetings or conferences need not be impeded by their physical limitations. Even employees with vision impairments may be able to participate fully in virtual worlds, as there are people working on technologies to make this happen (White, 2009).

There are numerous decisions organizations will need to make to introduce avatars into their culture. There may be a push to limit how much a person can customize their avatar in an enterprise environment in order to adhere or comply with corporate policies. The trade-off of this decision is the risk of less opportunity for an emotional connection between the employee and his avatar. Ultimately, it benefits the organization for employees to embrace and identify with their virtual counterparts. Any policy decisions that limit the opportunities to forge those connections should be made with caution, as they seriously jeopardize the likelihood that employees will embrace their avatars, and in turn may jeopardize the learner's connection to the immersive environment.

As avatars start to become another way that we represent ourselves, identity and trustworthiness will grow as an ethical discussion. There are many issues around trust and virtual identity that organizations will encounter when developing a virtual work-place environment. Questions that will need to be addressed by organizational policy, if not eventually by the courts, may include:

- Are an avatar's actions equal to an employee's actions?
- How are human relations policies applied in virtual environments?
- What are acceptable limits of self-expression by avatars in the virtual environment?
- How can you trust that the avatar you are interacting with is the person you believe him to be?

In 2007, *Science* magazine published an article on avatars regarding identity and trustworthiness, and tried to explore some of these issues. Building trust is inherent in the development of relationships, including business relationships. Representing our-selves through avatars leads to a certain level of anonymity, This anonymity must be overcome to build the same kind of trusting relationships, as we do when interacting in the real world (Donath, 2007). Although there are no clear answers, organizations must think of the implications of alternate forms of identity as they develop policies on expected organizational behavior.

The future of avatars leans heavily on a key developmental issue for virtual envi-ronments in general: interoperability. In short, the development of a single avatar that can be used in multiple environments would help users to more strongly develop their digital identity and prevent them from having to develop multiple avatars to represent themselves on multiple platforms. This is particularly important for business uses where identity, relationship building, and developing a professional reputation could be strengthened by a single, consistent identity that an employee has "bonded" with.

An avatar is a very complex creation and has the power to determine the success of a learner taking full advantage of immersive learning to the benefit of themselves and their organizations. When an avatar is selected to represent the learner in an immersive environment, your design should consider the ramifications of that pres-ence and leverage the psychological connections to your advantage.

USER EXPERIENCE

Once you have determined the performance goals, established the story line, and iden-tified the characters, you're ready to start defining the user experience for your immer-sive learning design. Think about the user experience as everything that the learner does, or is required to do, to interact in the environment from beginning to end. The user experience is what creates (or in some cases, can take away from) the level of immersion that the learner feels while engaging in the experience.

Start with the goal: What should people be doing differently or better, and how would they practice this skill to get better? Then, how can you recreate that experience through your story line, characters, and the technology that you are using to create the experience? The next chapter will cover technology selection in more detail, but you should be starting to make some technology decisions as part of the user experience design. For example, if one of the performance objectives is to have learners decrease their customer service call resolution time, how can you recreate an environment that mirrors the actual performance environment as closely as possible? Can you use the actual software, a training sandbox version, or will you need to recreate the functionality of the customer service system as part of the experience? Are customer service reps sitting at a computer answering calls, or are they working with live customers? These are the questions that need to be answered to determine which technologies can support creating an authentic practice environment.

A major consideration in designing an immersive learning experience is the learning curve for learners to figure out how to navigate in and engage with the immersive environment. Some technologies, like virtual worlds, have suffered in user adoption because learners become frustrated trying to figure out how to navigate before they even have a chance to engage with content. Although many platforms are simplifying the user experience, the cognitive overhead required to use any technology or platform for immersive learning should be one of the top technology selection and design decisions as you begin to focus on the user experience.

There are several strategies that designers may employ to plan and design the user experience in their immersive design. Flowcharts, storyboards, and use cases are all variations on a theme: What do learners do in your immersive environment and how do they do it? In most cases, you'll need to create all three of these components to fully define your user experience. Don't take shortcuts. The design of the user experience is where all questions of "and then what" must be answered. The designer passes off the design documentation for development, and the combined elements of the user flow, storyboards, and use case are where the answers to those questions are found. Each of these elements is focused on a different audience. The user flow should demonstrate to developers the programming logic, plus all of the interactions of features and functionality in the environment and how they respond to learner input. The storyboards are the story-line flow: Who does what when, and what happens when they do. The use case is written from the learner perspective and presents a "day in the life" view of interacting within the immersive environment. All three of these elements show the interrelationship between actions and consequences within your environment, but it is the three of them viewed in concert that creates the full picture of the user experience in the immersive environment.

USER FLOW

The user flow for immersive design should show all of the potential actions and decisions and their consequences within the story line, plus their effect on the progress toward success metrics and user options and outcomes in the environment. Creating the user flow is not for the weak of heart; it requires extensive thought of each element of the immersive learning environment and the actions that learners can take, decisions learners can make, and the range of outcomes associated with those actions. The user flow is the map of functionality, potential actions, associated consequences, and their relationship with each other that visually demonstrates the user experience.

What does a user flow look like? For immersive learning experiences, user flows typically end up looking like flowcharts on steroids. In the days before digital flowcharting tools, typical simulation user flows would take up several conference room walls. Now, flowcharting tools can help document the user flow, but care must be taken to visually demonstrate the interrelationships.

The user flow on the next page is for an immersive game designed by a graduate student and represents one level of an immersive learning game. This user flow demonstrates a fairly simple scenario-based simulation intended to help orient new users to a giant spherical kinetic learning environment called "Virtusphere." Because the performance goals are focused on mastery of movement within the "Virtusphere," the story line for this game provides context for practicing different actions like walking and running. The user flow shows actions and consequences for the limited set of options available to learners: Either complete the appropriate motions, or don't.

For many immersive learning experiences that are very open, that is the appropriate design strategy, since there is an almost unlimited set of "wrong" choices but only one or a small number of options that demonstrate progress toward achieving the performance objectives. In those cases, it is most important to focus on what constitutes progress rather than identifying what constitutes failure or nonprogress.

In addition to the flow diagram, the user flow should include a feature list for the immersive learning environment. For the development phase, this list will ensure the environment allows for the appropriate range of actions and decision making to emulate an authentic practice environment as closely as possible. The feature list is also the key to the user flow; all features and their interrelationship to the immersive environment should be represented in the user flow diagram.

SAMPLE USER FLOW

Game Components

The following graphics illustrate all components to be included in the game:

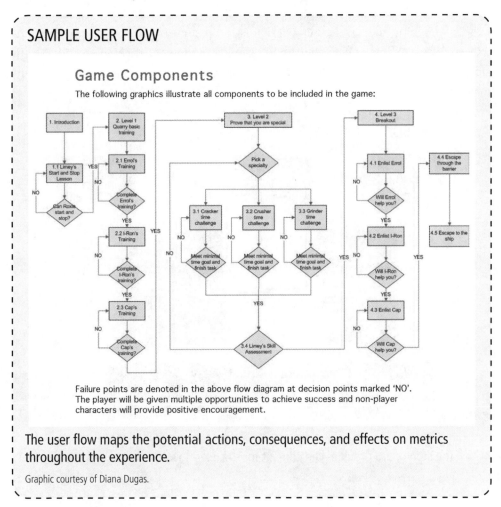

Failure points are denoted in the above flow diagram at decision points marked 'NO'. The player will be given multiple opportunities to achieve success and non-player characters will provide positive encouragement.

The user flow maps the potential actions, consequences, and effects on metrics throughout the experience.

Graphic courtesy of Diana Dugas.

STORYBOARDS

The user flow diagram shows the interrelationship of what happens in the immersive learning experience; the storyboards provide the context for that user flow. Storyboards are where the performance goals, content, story line, and characters come together. If you've created a comprehensive user flow, the storyboards are the "script" of the diagram, with all of the detail and dialogue that is not included in the visual representation of the flow. Think of the user flow as the table of contents and the storyboards as the pages in your experience, with each page mapping back to the user flow.

Storyboards come in all shapes and sizes. Some include graphics and some don't, some are structured in elaborate tables or templates, and some are simply written in prose with identifiers mapping the content to the user flow. The key to creating storyboards for your immersive learning design is completeness and consistency. Anything that you want to show up in your immersive learning experience needs to be in the storyboards; if the user flow is the blueprint of your design, the storyboards are the instructions on how to build it.

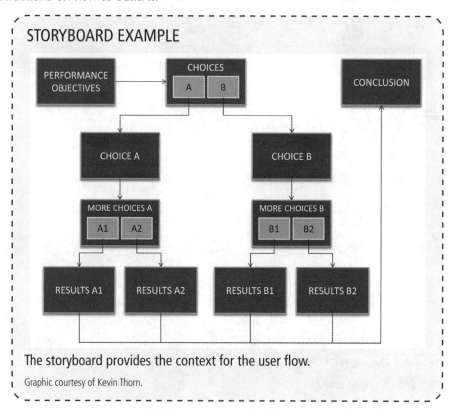

STORYBOARD EXAMPLE

The storyboard provides the context for the user flow.

Graphic courtesy of Kevin Thorn.

USE CASE

You've got your blueprint and you've put together your building instructions, but you still need to explain how you want people to use what you're building. That is the purpose of the use case. The use case walks you through your immersive learning design from the learner perspective. What happens first? What choices do I have the opportunity to make and what happens when I make them? Why is that important to me, the learner?

The use case helps you think through your design decisions from your target audience perspective. Writing from the perspective of your end users will help you identify what features and functionality might be important to them that you hadn't previously considered. Putting yourself in the end user's shoes also helps you refine your flow and storyboards to highlight the most important content.

I tend to write my use cases from a third-person perspective and create an end user character to explore the context in which the learners will be engaging in the immersive learning experience. Questions like "How long should learners expect to engage in the experience at a time?" or "How do learners know how much progress they've made?" are answered in detail.

The following example of a game use case was taken from graduate student Diana Dugas's game design document. The narrative of the experience from the end user perspective is the goal of the use case, and this simple example demonstrates how that writing style can "tell the story" of your immersive learning design.

PLAYER USE CASE

1.0 Introduction

Description:

Limey provides an introduction of the Quarry and explains that all of the workers must contribute to the production of diamonddust.

User Experience:

The game starts after the player steps into the Virtusphere (VS) and puts on the vr headset. The initial cut scene begins with a black screen which slowly lightens up to reveal a dimly lit alien environment. A large gray lump rock lumbers toward the player and begins to speak. The rock addresses the player as Roxie Cutter and introduces himself as Limey Stone; he proceeds to explain where the player is, what the player is and why. Limey asks the player to look around his cave. The player sees Limey, an opening at the opposite end of the cave and a glowing patch on the wall behind her. The player can hear popping and cracking sounds nearby and a low rumble at a distance.

1.1 Limey's Start and Stop Lesson

Description:
Limey teaches the player how to move in a heavy rock-shaped shell.
User Experience:
Moving in front of the player, Limey explains that before the player can leave the cave, she must first learn how to walk. Limey gives the player some tips and tricks on how to start moving and how to stop. He asks the player to copy his actions and gives supportive feedback. Since the player cannot talk or type, dialogue is triggered based upon the player's performance. When Limey states that he is pleased with the player's performance, the player says "Thanks! You are a good coach!" Limey responds with a joke about his other life. The level ends when Limey is satisfied with your basic skills and asks you to follow him out of the cave.

2.0 [Level 1] Quarry Basic Training

Description:
Limey directs the player to visit each of the quarry specialists to receive introductory training on a quarry skill.
User Experience:
Limey and the player stand outside of Limey's cave. When the player looks around, she sees that she is in a large pit. The walls are high but are terraced. To the right of Limey's cave is the source of the popping and cracking sounds, a sharp-edge gleaming rock form slamming into the face of the wall in a shower of sparks. In front of the cave is a large, uneven area with a large lumpy rock form rolling along what looks like a path. The form passes in front of them crushing the rocks on the path. To the left of the cave, a ramp goes into an odd-looking structure that spews sparkling dust up into the sky. High and low-pitched grinding sounds emanate from the building as well as a commanding voice. "New recruits! Fantastic! We might just meet our quota today."
The player turns to Limey and asks "What IS this place?" Limey responds with "Not now. We need to get production up. So follow me, let's get started."

The use case helps you think through your design decisions.

Graphic courtesy of Diana Dugas.

Because every immersive learning experience is different and specific, it's impossible to provide absolute guidance on how to know if your user experience elements are completely defined. That said, there are some questions that someone with no previous knowledge of your design should be able to answer after reviewing your user flow, storyboards, and use case:

- What is the purpose of the experience?
- What is the goal of the experience?
- What are the obstacles to achieving the goal?
- What are the mechanisms to overcome the obstacle?
- What do characters do?
- How do characters interact?
- What tools do you need to engage in the experience?
- Can the goal be accomplished by an individual, or do people have to work together? Do learners play as a team?
- How do you know you have won?

These questions are basic, but the devil is in the details. The details differentiate a user experience design that a developer can easily build into an experience that matches your vision and goals, from one where a developer needs constant support to build it, and it ultimately doesn't reflect your original intent.

Since what you are trying to build is complicated, you'll always have items pop up that need more clarification: functionality that needs to be tweaked and user flow that needs to be altered. Your final immersive learning environment will not, in all likelihood, match your user experience design elements exactly, and that's part of the iterative design process. In developer terms, think agile, not waterfall. Plan, plan, plan... then observe, listen, adapt, and improve.

5.
DEVELOPMENT: PUT IT TOGETHER

Although the main design responsibilities are in the analysis and design stages, immersive learning design should be an iterative process because of its focus on performance improvement. It's not as simple as presenting content, assessing for comprehension, and then checking the "learned" box. Performance is dynamic and variable, and so learning experiences that allow for performance practice should—as much as possible—be dynamic, flexible, and able to be adjusted over time. There are some design responsibilities and decisions that are important for immersive learning that affect the development, implementation, and evaluation stages of the design process.

DEVELOPMENT CONSIDERATIONS: IMMERSIVE LEARNING DESIGN

As part of your analysis, you collected information on your target audience, their technology familiarity, how they currently leveraged technology as part of their performance, and the context that they would be learning in. While those answers all shape the experience design, they also narrow down, and sometimes dictate, your technology selection and overarching experience structure.

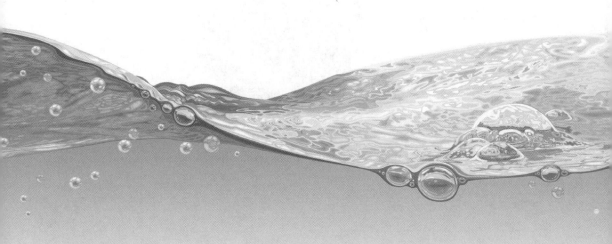

Because technology changes so quickly, it's not practical to list the specific technologies that can be used to develop immersive learning environments. Instead, this chapter will describe: the major categories of immersive learning designs as a starting point; the immersive technologies that can support your design decision; why you might select them; and their benefits and limitations.

The most highly recognizable design categories that fall under immersive learning design are games, simulations, and virtual worlds. However, there are two additional design strategies—alternate-reality games (ARGs) and 3-D immersive environments—with unique features that, while they overlap with other categories, differentiate these types of experiences enough as separate design categories.

To get started, here's a very simple definition of the differences between a simulation, a game, and a virtual world. A virtual world is a framework, an environment if you will. It's a place waiting for context and possibly content. A game is competitive or scored and the goal is to win (although for serious games, we're hoping something is learned in that quest for victory). A simulation is a realistic recreation of a process or task that allows learners to practice and experience realistic outcomes.

A 3-D immersive environment looks like a virtual world, but it has content and context and is not necessarily synchronous or multiplayer. An ARG is a game that takes the play experience out of a strictly digital environment and into the real world, allowing a story line to drive players to practice real activities as part of playing the game.

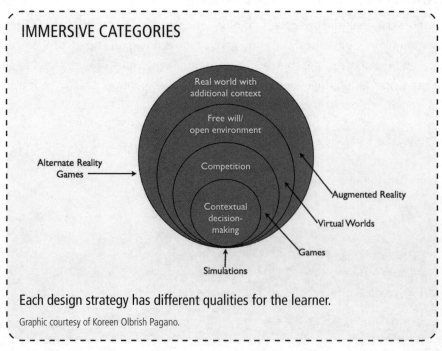

IMMERSIVE CATEGORIES

Real world with additional context

Free will/ open environment

Alternate Reality Games →

Competition

Augmented Reality

Contextual decision-making

Virtual Worlds

Games

Simulations

Each design strategy has different qualities for the learner.

Graphic courtesy of Koreen Olbrish Pagano.

Each design strategy may be more or less appropriate for your particular performance objectives, audience, and learning environment. Each design strategy has particular immersive technologies associated with them that may dictate whether or not it can be utilized. The following sections will provide guidance on the benefits and challenges associated with each design strategy.

GAMES

Sid Meier has described a game as "a series of interesting choices" (Rollings and Morris, 1999). Whole volumes have been written arguing over the definition of a game, and it is not my intent to replicate that here. Since there are a variety of games, from single-player card games like solitaire, to multiplayer board games, to team sports like football, to the more modern creation of technology-based games, it becomes difficult to create a concise description of what a game is. The *Merriam-Webster* dictionary defines a game as "a form of play or sport, especially a competitive one played according to rules and decided by skill, strength, or luck," and this seems like a solid basis for our purposes.

So what is a "serious game"? A quick search online returns lots of definitions, but my favorite is from *Wikipedia*: "Serious games are designed for the purpose of solving a problem" (2013).

While games have long been viewed as a tool for learning, focusing on games as a vehicle for solving a problem puts the emphasis on behavior change and performance improvement. This differentiates serious games for learning from many of the simple review "game show" games used for knowledge checks of assessment in many training environments. In particular, these types of serious games—immersive learning games—focus on players practicing skills in a game context.

ALTERNATE-REALITY GAMES

Alternate-reality games (ARGs), also called "pervasive games" or sometimes referred to as "transmedia storytelling," are designed to combine real life and digital game play elements. Typically, ARGs are "tracked" online, but the actual game play consists of real-life activities. There are many entertainment-based examples (*i love bees, The Lost Experience, Numb3rs Chain Factor*) and examples of ARGs for serious purposes (*Urgent Evoke, World Without Oil*). A new area of focus is how ARGs can be leveraged for learning. I've seen a lot of confusion in the term ARG—some people use "alternate-reality games" and "augmented reality games" interchangeably. Alternate-reality games, however, refer to game play that integrates real life and online game play; augmented reality games refer to games where there is a technology overlay on reality that contributes to play (think the first-down line on televised football games). What makes this even more confusing is that augmented reality technology can actually be used as part of an alternate-reality game. To keep it straight in your mind, think about the actual meaning of the words: alternate refers to a "different" reality, in the case of ARGs, a different story line that you're following as part of the game. Augmented means enhanced, which can be seen through the additional data layer that augmented reality technologies provide.

FOR OVERLAPPING DESIGN STRATEGIES, SEE ARIS/DOW DAY CASE STUDY ON PAGE 157.

It's difficult to make generalizations of what an ARG is or looks like for learning. Just as there are an unlimited number of games and rules for game play, the same is true for ARGs. Designs could range from something very simple (like a scavenger hunt) to something very complex (such as large-scale, problem-based learning leadership development). There are, however, some basic design principles and lessons learned as we have designed more and more ARGs for corporate learning.

- **Design is the key:** Just as with any game, ARGs are most successful when they are designed for the type of play and outcomes that both make them fun and engaging as well as focused on achieving the desired goals. This is not instructional design; this is game design with learning goals. A huge misconception is that because you've played games, you know how to design them. Don't underestimate the amount of time, energy, thought, and expertise that it takes to design a fun game, let alone a fun game that accomplishes your organizational learning goals.

- **Technology drives the experience:** You shouldn't underestimate the importance of the game design, but neither should you underestimate the importance of having a solid technology plan for driving and tracking the game play. Much of the basis of a good game is the mechanics—you can't play Yahtzee without dice or poker without cards. Technology enables game play and is an essential element of what makes an ARG successful.

- **What's your story:** Everyone loves a good story. The most successful ARGs embrace storytelling as a key element of the game play. For corporate training initiatives, the storytelling elements can either mirror real-life scenarios or be more of a fantastical overlay. Strategy for the story line should align with the design and objectives, but should not be overlooked as a critical aspect of the experience.

- **Stick to the point:** Yes, it might be fun to plan an ARG with a "Mission Impossible" theme, but it might not be appropriate for a game focused on team building. Make sure that your design is led by and focused on your learning objectives. Recognize that anything that doesn't support your goals might distract from them, and be strategic about what you focus on to reduce cognitive overhead.

- **Follow the rules:** People play games to win, and rules dictate what you need to do to win. Part of the complexity of game design is setting rules of play to balance game play at the sweet spot between "too hard" and "too easy."

- **Play to learn, not learn to play:** Beware of designing game play rules that are so complex that there's a significant learning curve to figure out how to play the game. Unless, of course, the goal of the game is to promote critical thinking skills...then it might be appropriate. But in general, ARGs should be designed with clear rules of play to help players focus on the content and help them accomplish the learning goals instead of figuring out how to play or win the game.

- **Should you keep it on the down low:** In the past, part of the intrigue and appeal of ARGs was that they were secret or subversive, which created an atmosphere of being "in the know." For learning, you probably don't want your training experiences to be secret, but it might not be a bad idea to think about how you can still create that feeling of subversiveness. Secret clues, bonuses, and secret codes are all examples of ways that you can create a "secret" feel to game play.

SIMULATIONS

Simulations, as opposed to games, seek to replicate some aspect of reality at some level of detail. It may be how to use the flight controls on a plane, how to conduct a successful sales call, or even how to conduct a surgical procedure. But a simulation is reality-based. Games are not bound to reality, although they may be designed to emulate the real world, like a simulation.

Simulations were designed to provide a risk-free environment for complex decision making. Model-based simulations, like a flight simulator or a financial simulation, can demonstrate how minute decisions can have immediate and long-term consequences. For scenario-based or soft skill simulations, interpersonal interactions are "scored" to provide feedback in the style of employee or client satisfaction. For any type of simulation, answers are not typically "right" or "wrong," but instead must be considered in context of the decision-making environment. When learners participate in simulations, they understand the complexity and consequences of decisions better, and it has been shown that their behavior change has increased (Holton, 2010). Games have clearly defined "win states" or victory conditions, a dynamic that is not required to be present in a simulation. Clark Quinn has argued that a "scenario is a simulation with goals" (Quinn, 2005). A pure simulation like Microsoft's Flight Sim is reality-based and has no preset way to tell if you've won. Wrap a goal into it, say, landing without crashing—and now you have a scenario.

FLIGHT SIMULATION EXAMPLE

Simulations can provide a risk-free environment for complex decision making.

Graphic courtesy of Softonic.

Simulations can have a great deal of freedom for the user, but only within certain boundaries. Simulations can be spatial and social, but those elements are not required to have a sim. While sims can run for a while, they are typically not persistent. While a virtual world can be a platform on which you could build a simulation, a simulation could not contain a true virtual world.

FOR SIMULATIONS WITH ACHIEVEMENTS, SEE GOV'T PROCUREMENT CASE STUDY ON PAGE 148.

3-D IMMERSIVE ENVIRONMENTS

What's open and 3-D like a virtual world, but with specific content goals, and not necessarily multiplayer and synchronous? You're right if you guessed 3-D immersive environments. 3-D immersive environments have all the look and feel—and benefits of presence—that learners get from virtual worlds, but they have context and content, and they aren't synchronous or multiplayer.

If you think this description sounds very much like many console or computer games, you're right. From RPGs to first-person shooters, many of the latest games are 3-D immersive environments where you are playing out a story line and working to achieve goals. So what's different?

3-D immersive environments bring together the player experience from virtual worlds, the realism of simulations, and the goal-based learning of video games into one hybrid experience. The world is real and the learner has something to do in it. Maybe the learner is expected to perform virtual surgeries, or handle negotiations with hostile civilians in a war zone. Maybe learners are expected to manipulate virtual molecules to replicate experiments in a virtual environment. Or maybe manipulate production processes to improve production times without decreasing quality in a virtual manufacturing environment before applying those changes in real life. 3-D immersive environments can replicate practically any environment, with the goal of immersing learners and allowing them to practice tasks virtually before they apply them in real life.

3-D IMMERSIVE ENVIRONMENT EXAMPLE

You are talking to Nicky Hammond whilst on the way to see the client.

Thinking Worlds is an example of a 3-D immersive environment.

Graphic courtesy of Caspian Learning.

VIRTUAL WORLDS

Chances are if you've heard of virtual worlds, then *Second Life* is the one you've heard of. Publicity of that magnitude has been both a blessing and a curse. On the one hand, the success and notoriety of *Second Life* have served to bring the idea of virtual worlds to the attention of many people who would never have heard of them otherwise. *Second Life* has also created an impression of virtual worlds that is not in line with what corporations think they may need to achieve their business goals, and that perception has created a barrier to their use.

VIRTUAL WORLD EXAMPLE

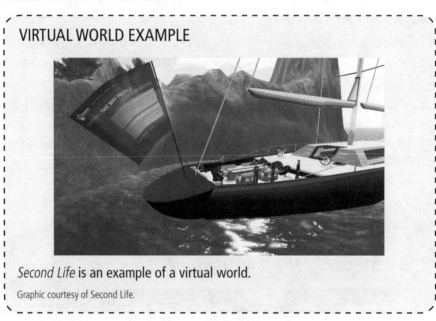

Second Life **is an example of a virtual world.**

Graphic courtesy of Second Life.

It is estimated that 803 million adults worldwide have a virtual world account, and around 500 million kids under 18 do too. All of this participation, however, hasn't garnered a definitive definition of a virtual world (KZero Worldswide, 2013). The lack of a settled definition is a challenge on a couple of fronts. Definitions help us manage our expectations of various enterprise systems. Clearly, a learning management system (LMS) would not be expected to deal with your accounting issues. So we need a definition to figure out what we can expect from and what we are looking for in a virtual world platform. Defining our expectations for what we want a virtual world platform to do also helps us describe what kind of technology base we may need to successfully implement a virtual world platform. Finally, settling on a definition for a virtual world will help us begin to think about what kind of learning opportunities we can actually design "in world."

Defining virtual worlds will also help to distinguish them from other activities, such as serious games and simulations, with which virtual worlds are often conflated. So we need to not only define what a virtual world is but also what it isn't. Defining these characteristics and differences help to determine which aspects make virtual worlds useful for learning, social networking, or collaboration.

Rather than try to define something that is still very much an evolving target, it might be best to approach this from an elemental perspective. So here are definitions of elements necessary for a virtual world, plus some of the other current definitions for comparison's sake.

- **"Spatial" environment:** Virtual worlds have the sense of a physical space, of "being" in a particular location. This isn't about one location specifically but rather is about a sense of place. One ongoing discussion centers on if virtual worlds need to be 3-D and while "true 3-D" may not be required, a sense of place is an essential element.

- **Avatars:** An avatar is your physical representation in a virtual world; it's you. You have control not only over what this avatar does but usually to some degree, what it looks like. Now, through the avatar, you are able to interact (communicate, move, react) in a digital environment, such as a virtual world. And while the avatar represents you in the virtual world, it does not have to have any similarity to how you look, act, talk, or generally appear to others in the real world. An individual has the opportunity to create an avatar to look and behave however that individual chooses.

- **Shared space:** Virtual worlds are, at their heart, social spaces—that is, they are spaces that you occupy with others usually using the space to work together toward some mutual goal. Both the variety and richness of ways that you can communicate with others in these spaces now includes text messaging, VoIP, and video. One of the interesting aspects of virtual worlds is that they allow for nonverbal communication as well through avatars. Gestures, movements, and expressions are all opportunities for communication with others in-world.

- **Interaction with the world/agency:** A defining characteristic for virtual worlds is the ability for users to have often unprecedented levels of control over their environment and the world. This "agency" goes beyond navigation and can extend from controlling how your avatar appears, to having user-generated content.

- **Context**: Simply put, there needs to be a reason for people to show up. Unlike a massive multiplayer online game (MMOG), virtual worlds don't have to have a story line or goals associated with participating in the world. Much of what happens in a virtual world mirrors what happens in real life: people respond to the events that surround them and those interactions build the context, or community. But there needs to be a reason for people to come into the virtual world in the first place. Whether it's for social or business reasons, virtual worlds must have a purpose.

- **Persistence:** In order for something to be considered a "world" there is a necessity that it exist outside of the influence of any individual person. In other words, a virtual world continues to exist, perhaps even to change, whether you are in the world or not. In this sense, a virtual world is like any physical location; it doesn't go away just because you're not there. You can leave the virtual world, but its presence is persistent for others who may visit, and it will be there whenever you choose to return.

Through these features, a virtual world is defined as a persistent online environment in which users, represented by avatars, can move and interact with the environment for some common purpose.

OVERLAPPING DESIGN STRATEGIES

This book is titled *Immersive Learning* because immersive learning is a design concept spanning categories of design strategies that have multiple overlaps and similarities. Can immersive learning be developed in 3-D, a virtual world, a game, or a 3-D immersive environment? Yes to all. Is immersive learning scored, a simulation, a game, or a 3-D immersive environment? Any of the above. Do ARGs and virtual worlds both need someone monitoring learners to guide the experience, give feedback, and keep people on track? Yes. The truth is, in many cases, there are more similarities than differences among simulations, games, ARGs, immersive learning environments, and virtual worlds. But regardless of the labels people apply, the design strategy—designing for authentic practice in a realistic context—is what binds all of these types of learning experiences into the category of immersive learning.

One thing to keep in mind is the difference between the platform, the technology, and the experience. A virtual world is a platform; a game is an activity or experience. A console is a technology; an ARG is an experience. A smartphone is a technology; a simulation is an experience. You can utilize any of these technologies for activities, but it is the design strategy built on a platform and delivered via technology that creates an immersive learning experience.

IMMERSIVE LEARNING AND E-LEARNING

Any learning experience delivered via technology can be considered e-learning. E-learning is the umbrella under which any of the items listed in this section could fall. Traditionally, however, e-learning is thought of as online (or computer-based) tutorials delivered to individuals and structured similarly to print tutorials, with the benefit of optionally including multimedia and automated assessment.

E-learning is useful in its accessibility: It may be available from any computer in any location throughout the world. It allows for scheduling flexibility: Students can complete e-learning at any time based on their schedules instead of attending classes at a specific time. E-learning can include rich multimedia experiences—video, audio, and other multimedia—to support learning experiences rather than traditional text and images used in print-based training. E-learning is also useful in that it can track user data, provide assessments to students, and automatically score and record the results of those assessments. It has the ability to provide feedback to learners in real time, and even has the ability to provide multiple content or learning pathways based on the results of the assessments that it provides. For example, if a student does not meet a minimum score, he may be asked to repeat more remedial material, while a student who reaches a certain target score may be presented with more advanced learning material.

So e-learning as defined above is content that can support immersive learning or could be integrated within it. Current innovations in immersive platforms include the seamless integration of 2-D and 3-D worlds, and most platforms allow links to supplemental materials, including more traditional, content-focused e-learning. To integrate within immersive learning, a learner could start taking a traditional e-learning course. She could then use immersive environments to debrief with other learners, attend a collaborative session, or practice applying the content in an authentic environment, before then returning to the traditional e-learning course to move on to the next concept. Rosetta Stone uses this model to teach a new language; learners are presented with content to learn new vocabulary, then synchronous language chats with fluent language speakers are offered to provide realistic practice and get learners speaking, not just listening and memorizing. This integration of content presentation through e-learning and immersive practice can facilitate the immediate application of new knowledge in context and bridge the gap between knowing and doing.

TECHNOLOGY SELECTION: RATIONALE

How do you pick which technology to use for your immersive learning design? Consider the performance goals, the audience, and the learning environment. There are often a few different technologies that might serve your purpose; your role is to identify the one that best meets your goals while best matching your development parameters. Above all, don't start by selecting a technology, unless you've only got one option. Always start with the analysis and then map your needs to the appropriate technologies, taking into consideration resources you will need to have available for development.

If you need an ultrarealistic re-creation of a process, a simulation might be the most appropriate design choice. If it's a re-creation of equipment use (for example, a flight simulator), you will likely have to custom build the environment; if it's a simulation of business decision making with financial implications, you likely need a model-based simulation to mirror the market dynamics and financial environment. If you need to create a scenario-based simulation, there are some standard development tools you may select from, or you may choose to create a custom build.

Typically, simulations are computer-based (not including live simulations, which are also immersive and extremely valuable for learning, but for the purposes of this book we're focused on technology-enabled immersion). Although console games with motion controls, such as the Nintendo Wii, have been used for some simulations—like virtual surgeries—in general, computers have been the primary technology selection for simulations.

If you have a complex skill that requires multiple, repeated rounds of practice until competency is reached, you may select a simulation, but you may also decide on a game. Because games are guided by rules and incorporate competition, they add features (such as options for multiplayer or competitive play, a scoring layer) that many simulations don't typically provide. Games don't need to be realistic and can be chosen for simple, discrete performance objectives, or for much more complex decision making. Games encourage players to learn over time, either through repetition and incremental improvement, or through increasing levels of difficulty as skill level improves.

Focusing on technology-centric games, you have various options for development tools. While custom-game platforms and engines are always an option, there are numerous game engines that can be leveraged for development of everything from simple 2-D games to complex 3-D immersive games. Console games can be designed to leverage either traditional console controllers, or use kinetic motion sensors to control your interaction in the game environment. Mobile games are among the fastest growing segment and appeal to an increasingly large audience as smartphones have become ubiquitous. Handheld game devices such as the Nintendo 3DSi have specialized in providing a mobile gaming platform and have integrated additional gaming features such as 3-D graphics and augmented reality gaming. Augmented reality capabilities are now available in most smartphones as well, providing new development tools to incorporate into your immersive design.

If your performance goals would benefit from allowing learners to practice using the actual tools they need to perform, then an ARG would be your best design strategy. ARGs provide a story-line context for practice and they apply a scoring structure to reward real activities, so it is an ideal design strategy when you have the ability for learners to practice in their real performance environment.

- - - - - - → **FOR AUGMENTED REALITY SOLUTIONS, SEE MILITARY MECHANICS CASE STUDY ON PAGE 157.**

Most ARGs will require you to integrate many tools in your development process, but usually these are tools the learners are already using on the job. You may use enterprise software systems such as email and voicemail for game characters to send messages to learners. You may leverage social media tools and social networking sites to communicate with players as well. Existing websites or intranet sites may be utilized, or you may need to create new webpages to develop the story line and contextualize the learning. For any ARG, you'll need a game engine to track the game play by learners; typically this is a website that learners can access from their computer or mobile device. There are a few organizations that provide ARG engines that can serve as the central portal for your game, or there are open-source platforms, or you could choose to develop a custom game engine.

One of the major considerations when designing an ARG is actually not a technical one. Because ARGs are dynamic and game play is monitored in real time, you'll need to ensure you have the human resource of a puppet master available to monitor and manage the game. While an ARG design strategy may be the best for achieving your objectives, the nature of the game play requires the puppet-master role; if that level of human management is not available for the duration of game play, another design strategy should be employed.

Because of the benefits avatars can bring to your immersive learning design, a 3-D immersive environment might be the best design strategy to employ. Learners have more control over their actions, with an openness not seen in many games and simulations. Successful applications of 3-D immersive environments might include insurance adjusters exploring a virtual home with fire damage, or police investigators collecting evidence at a virtual crime scene. In these examples, the context is important, but the actions of learners are open and exploratory.

There are a few options for creating 3-D immersive learning environments, but for most contexts you will likely need to build a custom environment on an existing platform. While costs have certainly gone down in recent years, 3-D assets are still more cumbersome to build than 2-D, especially in open environments. Although augmented reality and mobile apps may enable 3-D immersive designs to be more mobile, the other limitation is that these environments are primarily available through computers, and in some instances, game consoles. Increasingly, 3-D immersive development tools are becoming available with libraries of prebuilt environments or 3-D assets, but in these environments you get only a few options.

If you need people to interact with each other in real time in an open, exploratory learning environment, your best option is a virtual world. Virtual worlds allow you to build contexts within which learners can interact and explore with each other. Some virtual worlds even allow you to develop game experiences within the world, creating an interesting blend of open, synchronous learning and goal-driven practice.

There are several virtual world platforms available for development, but all have their strengths and weaknesses. Some platforms allow for less customization and user-generated content, focusing on the learner interactions as the main benefit of the environment. Other platforms are wide open and allow learners to not only be "residents" but also be builders. There are public platforms like *Second Life*, and there are many "closed" platforms that organizations can build out and make available only to selected audiences. Costs range as well, from platforms that are free or low cost, to enterprise-integrated platforms that may cost hundreds of thousands of dollars. Virtual worlds can be an amazing learning tool, but selection of the appropriate platform is dependent on the information you acquire during your analysis phase, as well as the commitment of the organization to integrating virtual worlds into their culture.

6.
IMPLEMENTATION: USE IT

IMPLEMENTING IMMERSIVE LEARNING

So you've designed it and you've built it. Will they come? Immersive learning experiences are new and unusual for most organizations. Be honest...how much actual practice is provided to your learners, let alone practice where what they do can be tracked? While people are used to playing video games and mobile games, most aren't accustomed to using those technologies to learn and practice things important to their education or job. In short, it requires a paradigm shift because their worlds (entertainment and work) are colliding. Suddenly, something that they used to do for fun now has implications that affect their future success. The challenge of immersive design implementation is to create an environment where learners feel safe practicing, see the value in the experience, and embrace the experience as an opportunity to improve their performance.

CULTURE

For immersive learning to be truly effective as a practice environment for performance improvement, it cannot be introduced as an assessment tool. Yes, the truth is that everything that learners do in the environment can be tracked and you could use that data to assess performance. But that would actually defeat the purpose of practice, and instead of creating an environment for incremental practice to improve performance, you would have created an elaborate assessment tool. Maybe that's what you want. But assessment alone does not improve performance; guided practice does.

Consider this: You're given a safe environment to practice in, a sandbox to explore the implications to all sorts of actions and decisions that you might never try in the real world. You see all the bad things that can happen. Or, you aren't really all that good at the tasks, but you go into the sandbox every day to practice and slowly you're getting better and better. Now, what if you're given that sandbox to practice in, but you're told that everything you do will be tracked and every decision you make will be seen by your manager. How does that change your behavior? You might decide to only go in and make the "right" decisions to prove you know what you're doing. If you're not skilled at the task, you might be hesitant to go in at all, for fear of consequences for your less-than-optimal performance. Certainly, the pressure of knowing that your practice is being evaluated changes the dynamic of your immersive learning experience, and changes your attitude of its value. When practice is evaluated, the practice is no longer for the learner; it is for the managers, the stakeholders, and the instructors.

To do immersive learning right, it needs to be about the learners. Practice needs to be practice, not assessment. Learners must have the freedom and support to fail.

It is extremely tempting to fall into the assessment trap. In order to preserve the purpose and value of an immersive learning experience, you must resist the temptation to make learning about tracking the process instead of about the outcomes. Failure and risk-taking are intimidating when you're under a microscope; instead, think of immersive learning as a safety net for exploration, and communicate that intent to your learners.

It's not just failure that should be supported; learning can and should be fun. How many learners in your organization actually look forward to training? (I'm guessing you have to think about it.) When people enjoy something, they want to do it more. Learning is always work, but it's work we enjoy. Easy games aren't fun...it's the challenging games that we want to beat that keep us playing again and again.

For people who dismiss games or immersive learning as "not serious learning," ask them if they have ever played a team sport, or any sport. How did they get better? Was it fun? What did they learn?

Part of the success of immersive learning experiences depends on the cultural support of the value of practice and the motivation to practice. Fun is a motivating factor and should not be dismissed from your tool kit. Humans are playful and curious and competitive. Immersive learning taps into these very human characteristics and leverages them for learning. It's not child's play to want to enjoy improving your skill; it's human. Embracing human nature in learning design will improve your learning and performance outcomes by creating a learning culture that supports practice to improve performance (Dirksen, 2011).

USABILITY

Inevitably, when talking about immersive learning design, people start throwing out the common objections:

- "I'm not a gamer."
- "I don't know where to go or what to do next."
- "This is too hard for people to figure out."
- "Our employees aren't technology savvy."

To which I say: Yes, you are. Yes, you do. No, it's not. And they are more savvy than you think…and they can learn. Stop designing to the lowest common denominator.

Educational research shows that tracking students into lower level courses actually reduces their chances for success. Lower expectations lead to lower results. Maybe surprisingly, the opposite also holds true. Lower-achieving students exceed expectations on their performance when they are put into advanced classes. When people set high performance expectations, people strive to achieve them. Even if they fall a bit short, they are able to do much more than if expectations were set lower (Kraft, 2013).

Stop setting low expectations of what your learners can do.

Everybody plays games. Maybe not video games, and that's OK. But we all play, and it's counterproductive to allow employees to disengage from practice because the format is new to them. Maybe you don't think of yourself as a gamer, but you could be, even if that's not how you self-identify. Maybe surprisingly, women over 50 make up approximately 14 percent of gamers, and this population is growing (Entertainment Software Association, 2011). How many of these women call themselves gamers? Probably not many, since the stereotype of that label is a guy in his late teens or early 20s playing a first-person shooter game in his parents' basement. Today's new gamers are more likely to be playing social games like *Words With Friends* or *Angry Birds* on their smartphones. I challenge anyone to tell me they don't play any games. We are all, by nature, gamers.

There is a caveat to all of my challenges to any usability objections: If you design a poor experience, people have every right to complain. Similarly, if you don't set appropriate expectations for learners, you will get confusion and resistance in exchange. If someone doesn't know where to go or what to do next in an immersive learning environment, there are two likely explanations: either the environment was designed poorly, or the learner is resistant to exploration. The user interface design, visual design, and navigational controls all contribute to the usability, but orienting your learners to the environment and setting expectations for how to explore and interact is equally important.

NONTRADITIONAL GAMERS

Who has never played a game?

Graphic courtesy of Gamersriot.com.

Assuming that your usability is designed well and you've appropriately oriented your learners to the environment, resistance to change or trying new things will likely manifest itself in usability objections. Be prepared during implementation to set your expectations high, to communicate the value of the experience and practice, and to recruit advocates who repeat the core value immersive learning brings to the learners and to the organization.

BEING THE PUPPET MASTER

For some immersive learning environments, the implementation phase consists of supporting learners "around" the environment, but for others, like ARGs and virtual worlds, implementation requires support inside the experience as well. The term "puppet master" is used in ARG design to describe the role of someone who guides and facilitates game play. Typically, the puppet master monitors player activity, communicates with the players to guide next steps, and is responsible for making adjustments during the course of the game as players engage in unexpected ways. In essence, ARGs require management throughout the experience, with the puppet master representing the role of facilitator and coach. Like the apprenticeship model of learning, the puppet master takes on the role of "master" to keep learners on track and provide them with any appropriate guidance or feedback. Depending on the structure of the ARG, puppet masters may be visible characters in the game and well known to players, or they may be "behind the curtain" and responsible for guiding the game experience that helps shape the learner's experience.

Virtual worlds may also require a puppet master–like role, although for virtual worlds, the puppet master is likely a participant in the environment, even if simply observing, coaching, and providing feedback on the interactions. Because virtual worlds are such open environments, the experience may require a puppet master–type role during implementation to ensure that learners stay on task and to help if questions arise. Similar to ARGs, it is a benefit if the person in this role is also an expert who can provide performance coaching and feedback in addition to simply guiding the game play.

WATCH THE PUPPET MASTER IN ACTION.
SEE EXTREME MAKEOVER CASE STUDY
ON PAGE 111.

Don't confuse the puppet master role with a help desk. The puppet master guides the experience and is most concerned with value the learners can gain from the immersive experience—they may not be able to help with technology questions or issues. In many cases, the puppet master may work in tandem with a technical support person who can serve to help players with any technical difficulties during the learning experience. This ensures the puppet master focuses on facilitation of learning and performance support.

ISSUES

Let's start with the biggest challenge in implementing immersive learning: not thinking big enough. Honestly, immersive learning provides an opportunity to revolutionize how organizations train their employees. Suddenly, companies can teach critical decision-making skills by demonstrating consequences. Dispersed workforces can bond and learn together. People can learn by doing, virtually. This requires a shift in thinking about training and learning on the part of organizations. In essence, learning can now be leveraged as a competitive advantage.

There is a danger in teaching employees how to think critically, at least for established hierarchies. Suddenly, your organization is much "flatter" and everyone has a more equal opportunity to contribute and communicate. Not only will learning structures have to be re-evaluated, but perhaps entire organizational structures. This isn't to say this will happen overnight. But companies who realize the potential of immersive learning must also be prepared for the revolution of ideas and smarter talent pool at their disposal.

A practical consideration for the integration of immersive learning as a curriculum strategy is the integration with other learning and knowledge management systems. The current openness of virtual learning environments has challenged our traditional thinking of knowledge management. However, the integration of learning structures like games and simulations allow for decision-tracking and completion acknowledgement through traditional database mechanisms. Companies must think through their needs for knowledge management as part of an immersive learning implementation to ensure that the proper information is being tracked, or not, for the best benefit of user and organization adoption.

In the past, standards like IEEE and SCORM limited the types of data that organizations could track in their learning management systems (LMSs). The types of data that these standards tracked made it impossible for organizations to know what to do with data from games and simulations. With new standards emerging, such as the Learning Experience API, learning experiences can be tracked in different ways and organizations can have a fuller, more descriptive snapshot of what people are learning in immersive learning environments.

7.
EVALUATION: KNOW IT WORKS

You designed it, you built it, you launched it…how do you evaluate it?

There are two ways to look this question: evaluating the immersive learning experience itself, or evaluating performance improvement. Ultimately, the success of any learning experience is whether or not learners' performance improves, so how you measure the success of practice should be how you are already measuring success of performance.

Attributing improved performance to the immersive learning experience is tricky because multiple factors affect performance. For example, a salesperson's skill may improve just as the market dynamics change for the product she is selling. Thus even if skill is improving, sales performance may be deteriorating because of market conditions. Similarly, a customer service rep might improve his response to customer issues because of an immersive learning experience, but a simultaneous upgrade to the customer relationship management software used in the call center may unnaturally inflate performance improvement.

As with any training initiative, it is often impossible to isolate the exact impact on behavior that a particular training initiative has. Often, it is in the combination of several metrics that the value can be discerned. In the case of the sales representative whose sales numbers decrease, looking at customer satisfaction or opinion data might reveal that customer satisfaction has increased while sales numbers have dropped. Looking comparatively across all competitors for sales numbers might also reveal

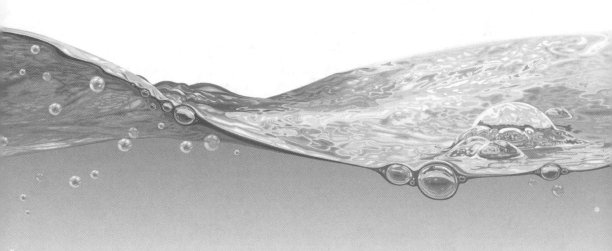

improvement: Has your market share increased, even while overall sales are decreasing? Identifying all of the data points that indicate performance and viewing them together will provide much more insight into the impact that immersive learning has on learner performance.

In order to measure improvement, you have to know where you started. Often, people say ROI can't be measured for learning initiatives, but the truth is that it can't be measured if you don't do the work up front: Identify the performance metrics you need to evaluate, and then take benchmark measurements to compare against future measurements. Evaluating performance and the impact of training should not be discussed after a training initiative has launched. If you want to measure value of any initiative, you need to design your experience to focus on the metrics that are valuable to you, then measure those metrics before the learning experience and again after.

One consideration for evaluating performance improvement as a result of immersive learning is collecting comparative data of audiences who have gone through the immersive learning experience with those who haven't. When implementing immersive learning for the first time, a pilot group is often selected to go through the experience and provide feedback before the full launch. Collecting the performance data for the pilot test group in comparison to their peers may provide comparative data to show immersive learning's value.

Another consideration is evaluating performance within the immersive learning environment as an additional data point or benchmark for performance improvement. When activities are performed through technology, every action can be tracked and data can be collected and aggregated. Immersive learning experiences allow you to collect data on all kinds of learner interactions and decisions that demonstrate a parallel to their real-life performance. When evaluating immersive learning, compare real-world performance measures to "in world" performance measures both before and after the learning, so the data points can help you see the effect of the immersive learning practice.

Immersive learning doesn't fit neatly into traditional grading or score-tracking measurement tools. Previous standards like SCORM and IEEE are not sufficient to measure what happens in environments like games and virtual worlds. There is no "final assessment" that will likely capture what learners will do differently, even if they demonstrate that they know what they need to do. For this reason, identification of the critical performance metrics as you are designing the game will dictate the data you are collecting and tracking. Creating a robust database and determining the types of reporting data to extract from the database you will need for your evaluation should be part of your design and development processes.

Besides behavioral and performance outcomes, the other metric that will be critical for evaluation is the time that players are investing in practice in the environment. By comparing "time in environment" to performance outcomes, you will be able to determine how much immersive learning practice roughly translates into how much performance improvement. In other words, you may be able to determine if one hour of immersive practice is sufficient to improve performance, or if players must invest 10 hours to achieve the desired results.

SCORING/SUCCESS MEASUREMENT

The most important question to ask yourself as you begin to think about scoring and success measurement is: How is success measured outside of the environment?

Often, the answer to that question isn't so simple. Take leadership training. How do you know someone is an effective leader? You might answer that the most important factor is the financial success of the organization. You might think employee satisfaction scores are the best indicator. You might cite reputation, or outward recognition, or maybe customer satisfaction. You could rightfully assert that stakeholder satisfaction, whether it's executive leadership, board members, or stockholders, is what matters most. The truth is, being a successful leader requires success in most, if not all, of these areas. Whatever your performance goals are for your immersive learning experience, the key is to identify all of the success metrics that contribute to the full measurement of success in the real world, then recreate and incorporate those metrics into your immersive learning design.

There are two parts to scoring that you must consider in your design: what data are collected in the environment to measure success and how that success is reported back to the learner. Identifying the success metrics and incorporating the data collection into your design is critical to evaluating learner performance and improvement. Think about what you need to track and how you can track it through the technology available to you. This is another factor that affects technology selection, as you can't evaluate improvement in performance if you're not able to collect data that demonstrates those improvements.

Once you know what data you need to collect, there are implications of how to collect it, or aggregate it. Are scores or success measures assigned to individual learners, to teams, or to both? For multiplayer experiences that allow teams to practice collaboration, team success metrics may be more important than individual performance, but you may still want to reward individual team members for exemplary performance.

Time is another critical parameter of scoring. Is speed a factor to success, and if so, how do you reward for timing? Scores may decrease over time, or you may choose to award extra points to the first learners to respond in a multiplayer environment. If time is measured through your story line, learners may only be rewarded at certain time intervals as tracked through the story line, which may affect your feedback strategy to prevent learners from going too long without performance feedback. Players may also be rewarded for how many times they accomplish a task within a specified time frame. In all of these instances, time is an essential element of the performance goal and should be emphasized as part of your design.

Once you've considered what data elements need to be collected and how they contribute to assessment of performance, you must consider how to share those success measures with learners throughout the experience. There are multiple ways to communicate success, but three main categories are a good starting point to consider when establishing your design: story-line feedback, success metrics, and achievements.

STORY-LINE FEEDBACK

Every decision that you make throughout your day has consequences, big and small. That's the story-line feedback in your life. You make people happy or sad. You are sometimes rewarded, sometimes disappointed, and sometimes decisions you make have unintended or unexpected consequences. In your story line, you can build in these types of feedback through character interactions and reactions to how you decide to act, to mirror what might happen in real life under the same circumstances. This story-line feedback should reflect the positive or negative, so there are sometimes conflicting results of the learner's actions in the environment. For example, the learner may choose to make a project team work over a weekend to hit a deadline and make a customer happy, but the other result is a very unhappy project team. The characters and story line can be an effective way to communicate performance feedback in the environment and help contextualize the corresponding success metrics, which are often a score or range that don't specifically provide feedback as to why a metric improved or suffered because of a decision.

SUCCESS METRICS

Success metrics are important for a reason: People like to see they are moving forward and that their actions have consequences, good or bad. For your immersive learning environment, you'll likely have at least one success metric indicator, which may be as simple as a persistent progress bar that shows incremental progress through the environment. You may have several success indicators that show a satisfaction rating, monetary objectives, or maybe simply a score. Think about your success metrics and how they could be visually represented for constant feedback to your learners, as an orientation to where they are progress-wise in the environment and in some instances, to compare their performance against a standard or to their peers.

ACHIEVEMENTS

The purpose of achievements should be to reinforce the performance and learning goals within your environment by adding an additional layer of feedback, or providing rewards for secondary or lesser performance goals. While your success metrics may indicate whether you win or lose, you may still win for "Miss Congeniality" and for some learners, that's a motivating achievement.

NERD BADGES

You can win badges, which are motivating achievements.

Graphic courtesy of Underconsideration.com.

As a game designer, I have a complicated relationship with the word "gamification." When game dynamics are applied to reinforce best practices and the learner's desired behaviors, that's great. When game dynamics are applied to reinforce desired consumer behaviors, I'm not such a big fan. In addition, slapping extrinsic reward structures on behaviors that people are intrinsically motivated to do can actually decrease their motivation to perform those behaviors long-term (Pink, 2011). As someone who values long-term behavior change, extrinsic rewards can become counterproductive to performance improvement.

While over-simplified reinforcement models are often confused with games because of the term "gamification," there is a place for achievements and badges as a reinforcement, feedback, or success indicator in immersive learning. For example, a procurement game concept was designed for a government agency as a scenario-based experience that challenges you, in the role of a contract officer, to make the right decisions about project bidding and contract types. While learners will benefit from and be rewarded for making the appropriate decisions, having them experience the consequences of incorrect decisions is also valuable.

FOR LOOKING AT DATA TO SHOW PROGRESS, SEE HEALTHSEEKER CASE STUDY ON PAGE 119.

To encourage replay ability and have learners explore all of the good and bad decisions in the game, achievement badges are used to reinforce certain decision paths, mistakes, and patterns (while adding some humor and elements of fun). For example, if you make decisions that make the program management office really happy at the expense of getting the best financial deals, you can win the "Everybody Loves Raymond" badge. Alternately, if you are exceptionally good at saving the most money but at the expense of your relationships with program managers, you can be awarded the "Everybody Hates Chris" badge.

SECTION 3
EXAMPLES OF
IMMERSIVE LEARNING

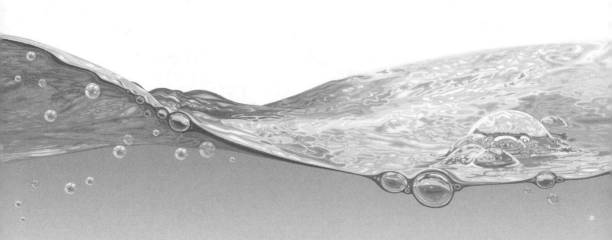

8.
CONTEXTUALIZED LEARNING

If someone wants to learn to play golf, they can sit in a classroom and hear golf pros tell them how to stand, how to hold a club, how to swing the club, and so on. They can watch videos of how to hit the ball. They can read about the appropriate clubs to choose for the various situations encountered on the golf course. However, they will never learn as much in the classroom or by reading a book as they would learn on the golf course: A person tries to hit a golf ball with an actual club while an instructor shows them how to hold the club, how to swing the club, how to select the club, and then provides specific feedback following the swing on what the individual did right and how they could improve on future swings. When learning a new skill it is perhaps best to learn while fully immersed in the environment where the application of that skill is appropriate.

IS READING ACTIVE?

Not so much.

Graphic courtesy of Shutterstock.

IS PLAYING ACTIVE?

Yes.

Graphic courtesy of Shutterstock.

Organizations are faced with the same challenge. It's not easy to learn most skills by reading a book, attending a lecture, watching a video, visiting a website, and so on. For many skills, the best way to learn is to practice them. It is often difficult or impossible to do this, at least without risk. For example, the best way for a salesperson to learn different selling skills may be to actually go out and practice selling things to customers. The problem with this approach is that companies cannot afford to risk losing an important sale or customer to allow an employee to practice. Customers aren't typically willing to allow a salesperson to come into their office to practice selling something as it may waste their time and doesn't provide much of value in return. As a result, the salesperson either needs to tag along with another salesperson and learn through observation or she needs to learn selling skills from books, online, and so on. Either of these options is less effective for engaging the learner than actually performing the skill or task, and both options leave out a critical element of performance improvement: practice. It is possible to try to simulate a sales experience by having another employee or trainer act as a customer. These role plays may be more effective but still have the limitation that the learner is not immersed in the environment (not to mention role plays are usually between peers with similar skill levels, and peers are not able to give appropriate coaching or feedback). Therefore, learning may take place under less than ideal situations and the learner may not effectively learn all the skills he needs to learn.

IMMERSIVE LEARNING SOLUTION

Immersive learning offers an authentic practice environment without risk to either the employee or the company and its business relationships. In returning to the example of the salesperson, rather than trying to have one employee provide training to another in an office setting or over the telephone, both employees could enter the immersive environment in a typical customer location or sales territory. The salesperson would be asked to sell a product to a virtual customer whether that customer avatar is a real person for multi-user environments or simply a character in the story line. Because the virtual environment resembles a typical sales location and the customer looks and behaves like a customer, it is much easier for the salesperson to become immersed in the environment and behave as they would in the real world, allowing for practice without risk of mistakes affecting the company.

It's not enough to be immersed in an environment to learn; that's simply the back-drop for the learning experience. The real opportunity for immersive learning is a shift away from content and toward context. What does this look like? Many examples can be seen in the gaming industry in massive multiplayer online games (MMOGs), in seri-ous games, and in simulations. These more immersive designs provide objectives in context. Virtual worlds provide a platform for practice, coaching, and feedback, real-time and in context. Mobile games and ARGs challenge players to interact with the real world to extend their learning and provide opportunities for synthesis of knowledge and skills through practice.

What does contextualized immersive learning look like? There are lots of ways to contextualize learning in either real world or authentic digital environments. Based on their audience and performance objectives, organizations may select various ways to engage learners in an immersive, contextualized experience. The following case stud-ies demonstrate how some organizations have designed contextualized learning to meet their goals and objectives. Case studies represent a wide range of audiences, environments, and contexts, as well as design strategies to show how widely immer-sive learning principles can be applied.

CASE STUDY: ELMWOOD PARK ZOO

Zoos and museums are not traditionally marketed as learning institutions because their primary mission is viewed as displaying collections of artifacts or animals. But they have recently begun to reflect a change in attitude toward education, becoming educational institutions in their own right. This change of mission can be seen in the wide array of educational opportunities offered by the largest of these institutions, such as home-school workshops, evening lectures, and programs for school and com-munity groups.

However, much of the education that actually happens in these informal science environments takes place out in the zoo, or on the museum floor, as visitors interact with an exhibit interpreter or educator. In fact, exhibit interpretation is one of the strongest tools for informal learning in these environments. Interpreters stand by as knowledgeable and accessible resources for a curious public, potentially providing an interaction that can elevate a visitor's experience from browsing to engaged learning. Unfortunately, in smaller institutions, a lack of funding may place exhibit interpreters outside the scope of potential offerings. In these cases it becomes extremely important for an institution to come up with creative ways to engage the public with its exhibits.

At one such institution—Elmwood Park Zoo in Norristown, Pennsylvania—an alternate reality game was recently run as an attempt to engage visitors beyond their natural tendencies. Sometimes people only see the zoo as a checklist of animals to see. The alternate reality game's goal was to motivate visitors to interact with the animals in the exhibits in new ways. The primary audience at the zoo was families with small children, most of whom became zoo members and returned to the zoo more than once a month. Because of this, the game needed to not only engage the families as a whole, with no real time constraints, but also be replay able so that zoo members could play each time they visited. It also needed to function with a minimum of staff intervention—in other words, the game needed to be self-contained and self-guided.

ELMWOOD PARK ZOO TEXT INTRODUCTION

NEW TEXT FROM
ELMWOOD PARK ZOO:

Welcome to the Elmwood Park Zoo!

Elma Wood, an EPZ biologist, is out wandering the world, looking for new species of animals, and she needs your help!

She has found some evidence that there is a new species nearby - but she hasn't seen it yet. She needs you to watch the animals here, and send her an idea of what she should be looking for!

Elma Wood, the fictional biologist, interacts with zoo visitors.

Graphic courtesy of Melissa Peterson.

The game focused on observation, creative output, and mystery or clue-based game play. Families played the role of sketch artists who help a fictional biologist, Elma Wood, who is out in the world searching for new species. Groups discovered that Elma recently found the tracks and evidence of what she thinks is a new species, but she has not yet seen this new species. Elma monitored the families during their zoo visit, and sent them messages when she noticed something that reminded her of the new species. The gamers were encouraged to observe the animals, their behavior, and the zoo habitat, and take notes if they wished. At the end of their visit, each family member got a chance to draw what the new species might look like, and where it might live, based on their observations.

ELMWOOD PARK ZOO TEXT ALERTS

NEW TEXT FROM
ELMWOOD PARK ZOO:

She is going to alert you through this phone when you are near an animal at the zoo which is like the animal she is looking for!

You should watch it closely, and may take notes if you'd like, so that you can send Elma a correct sketch later.

Elma gives out missions.

Graphic courtesy of Melissa Peterson.

The clues which Elma sent were generic, asking the families to observe the mouth and teeth shapes of whichever animal they were standing near, or to observe other adaptations (such as feet shapes, type of skin, type of fur). This allowed the game to be played without a set path through the zoo, so that families could visit their favorite animals without affecting game play. It also allowed the game to end with multiple correct answers for the final drawing, maximizing replay ability. This also allowed each player to participate at whatever level they were most comfortable and capable—a younger child's limited understanding was just as valid a final result as the more detailed drawings created by their older siblings.

Gaming groups carried a small pad of paper that served as a prototype for a hand-held device. The device was the method of communication between Elma and the group. For prototyping purposes, a facilitator, using sounds from a real cell phone, alerted the family groups when Elma was contacting them. Elma contacted the groups two to three times during their visit, to tell them they should observe a nearby animal, as it has some similarities to the new species. While observing the animal, the players noted their observations, using their pad of paper. When prompted for their sketch, players were given a set of conclusions Elma had come to, based on which animals they were told to observe. The conclusions included information about what the animal eats, where it lives, and what temperature it prefers. The players then created a sketch of the mystery animal, to aid Elma in identifying the animal when she finally sees it.

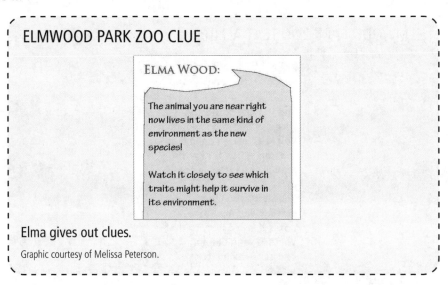

ELMWOOD PARK ZOO CLUE

ELMA WOOD:

The animal you are near right now lives in the same kind of environment as the new species!

Watch it closely to see which traits might help it survive in its environment.

Elma gives out clues.

Graphic courtesy of Melissa Peterson.

In the end, there were many clear signs that the game was functioning to further engage the visitors and create a greater understanding of animal adaptations. During the sketching, many of the players spent a great deal of time naming their animals and telling the facilitator about what their mystery animals ate and where they lived. While exploring the zoo, visitors spent (on average) double the amount of time engaging with the game-flagged exhibits compared to the rest of the exhibits they visited. Finally, even the youngest players were able to draw animals that showed understanding of at least one or more of the conclusions that Elma drew about the new mystery species. All of this was accomplished with minimal use of mobile technology, supported by paper and pencil and an engaging narrative.

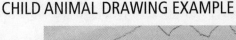

CHILD ANIMAL DRAWING EXAMPLE

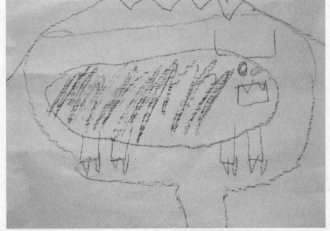

Even the youngest players could draw animals that showed understanding of the mystery species.

Graphic courtesy of Melissa Peterson.

CASE STUDY: GOVLOOP

When Steve Ressler founded GovLoop, a web portal for government workers to connect with each other, he faced a challenge. How do you get members of the GovLoop site to learn about all of the community features available to them? The content of GovLoop was extensive and rich, and members got the most value from connecting and interacting with each other. But the challenge was helping people learn about all of the resources available and getting them engaged fully with the site and each other.

While "gamification" is often a term used to describe creating a reward system to drive consumer behaviors, more and more organizations are looking at how to reward behaviors to encourage exploration and learning.

Such was the case with GovLoop. To encourage members to explore the site, engage with resources, and interact with other members, a rewards system was included in the site to incentivize behaviors that GovLoop wanted to see from their membership.

One of the key design strategies for the GovLoop site was to provide achievements for members engaging in desired behaviors, but to also create an end point to work toward. While some gamified experiences have no real end, and so often result in people losing interest and withdrawing from the very behaviors you want to encourage, GovLoop created a power user ranking that creates an end point. For a member whose behavior is motivated by garnering status, GovLoop's achievement system created a subtle reinforcement that explicitly revealed how Ressler hoped he would learn about and participate in the community.

For Ressler, creating the rewards system to encourage immersion in GovLoop was a success. Although some people don't pay attention to the achievements at all, for those that do, it provides a context for exploring the Govloop site and for participating in the robust community. It also provides metrics for participation that Ressler can look at to analyze how different members participate. Then, based on the activity and interests that are revealed through members' achievements, Ressler can use that information to shape future growth of the site.

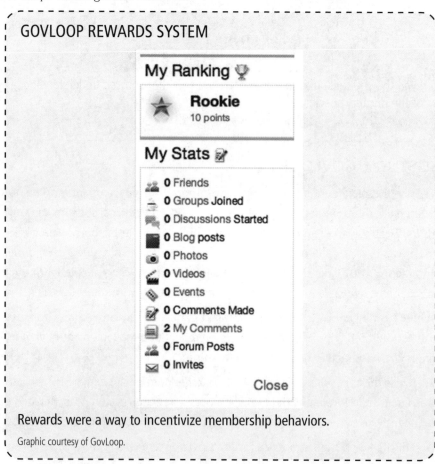

GOVLOOP REWARDS SYSTEM

Rewards were a way to incentivize membership behaviors.

Graphic courtesy of GovLoop.

9.
SERVICE SKILLS

Customer service and sales professionals are the face of many organizations; they interact with customers to drive sales and business success. Consider the following statistics on customer service from the article "20 Customer Service Statistics for 2001":

- It costs four to five times more to bring in a new customer, than it does to keep an existing one.
- 86 percent of people say they've stopped doing business with a company because of just one bad customer service experience (up from 69 percent in 2007).
- 60 percent of consumers say they will pay more for a better customer service experience.
- 81 percent of companies that measure customer service are outperforming their competition.
- A dissatisfied customer will tell between nine and 15 people about the experience.
- For every customer complaint, there are 26 others who feel the same way but remain silent.
- 91 percent of unhappy customers will not willingly do business with your organization again...ever (Zaibak, 2010).
- 66 percent of Americans are willing to spend an average of 13 percent more with companies they believe provided excellent customer service.
- 55 percent of consumers have "bailed" somewhere in the buying process because of poor customer service (Echo, 2012).

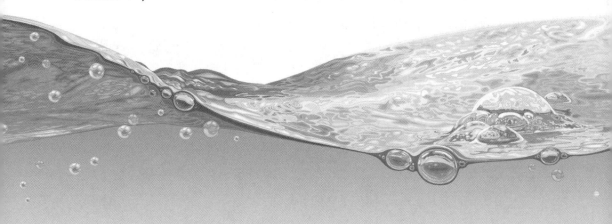

These statistics are only referring to customer service; sales skills directly affect a company's bottom line. With the Department of Labor and Statistics forecasting more than 2.6 million customer service representatives and more than 1 billion sales professionals by the year 2018 in the U.S. alone, the need to find ways to teach and improve service skills has never been greater (Lacey and Wright, 2010).

IMMERSIVE LEARNING SOLUTION

How do you teach someone to sell something? How can you get better at dealing with complex customer issues? The truth is, some people are naturally better at dealing with service situations, but that doesn't mean they can't improve. It also doesn't mean that people who aren't inherently gifted service providers or salespeople can't learn how to be successful. The key is practice.

Because immersive learning provides risk-free practice environments, it makes for an ideal format for organizations that want to improve their service skills. These organizational service skills could be face-to-face customer interactions, or phone or Internet sales and support. When you give learners not just the steps they need to take, but also opportunities to practice thinking through the logic behind those steps, they will become more agile in successfully navigating each unique situation that arises. Learners will not only know what they need to do in live customer interactions, but they will now have the experience and confidence to improve their customer interactions and outcomes.

The following case studies show how different organizations have designed immersive learning opportunities for their employees to practice their service skills in context: requiring them to leverage product knowledge, navigate internal resources to answer customer questions, and correctly respond to issues based on their knowledge of the customer, products, and processes necessary to be successful.

CASE STUDY: QUE SYRAH, SYRAH FOR CONSTELLATION ACADEMY OF WINE

The business of wine is as complex and vast as the many varieties of wine available today. The Constellation Academy of Wine offers the most complete training available for wine and hospitality professionals. They ensure that everyone from sales staff to sommeliers have impeccable knowledge of everything related to wine, so they can share with their customers to offer the best products to consumers.

Cheryl Hall of The Constellation Academy of Wine was tasked with improving the performance of more than 350 field sales managers in selling Constellation brands and positioning those products effectively among competitors. She chose to implement an ARG to tackle the challenge.

The Tandem Learning design team worked with Cheryl to create an experience where learners practiced data analysis, relationship building, and other selling techniques, all with a realistic but fictional hotel customer. The ARG narrative described characteristics of the hotel, including specific target customers, room descriptions, menus, wine lists, and sales data. Learners interacted with customer characters that were introduced and developed through the story line. During the three-week long exercise that culminated in their national sales meeting, events and circumstances that are commonly encountered in customer sales scenarios were presented to learners, requiring them to make decisions about appropriate actions and next steps in the fictional hotel account.

There were some lessons learned along the way. Constellation Academy of Wine had never implemented a game for learning before; in fact, they hadn't even implemented much e-learning. The executive management team was supportive, but cautious; their sales force was mainly in their 40s and 50s and the executive team wasn't sure how receptive they would be to playing a game to learn. Because of this concern, there was much discussion of the difficulty level of scenarios, which resulted in the design being simplified to ensure that players didn't find the experience too difficult to navigate. However, upon completion of the game, much of the feedback was that players actually wanted the scenarios to be more complicated and difficult; they liked the challenge of trying to figure out the best response to each situation and trying to practice the full complexity of handling customer interactions.

Another unexpected interaction was with the non-player characters (NPCs) in the game. As part of the story line, the characters in the ARG each had Facebook pages that provided players with more information on each of their customers. The characters posted information on their facebook pages for players that provided clues to the sales reps so they could make appropriate decisions. While the design was focused on characters communicating out to the players, Facebook pages allowed for people to post to characters' walls. Players began conversations with the characters and asked specific questions to get more information to make better-informed decisions. What started out as a one-way communication became a conversation. The puppet master's role was expanded in response to this interaction to ensure player questions and comments were responded to in a timely manner.

PLAYER FACEBOOK PAGE

Players interacted with Facebook characters in the ARG.

Graphic courtesy of Tandem Learning, a division of Ayogo Games.

The entire salesforce had Blackberry smartphones, so one of the technological benefits of using the ARG was that it was designed to play both on a computer or via a mobile device. Because there were internal sales representatives and external salespeople, having the game available on mobile devices was intended to level the playing field.

Two weeks into the game play, however, it was clear that three of the teams were so far ahead of the others that there was no way any other teams could catch up before going into the live game-play experience planned for the national sales meeting. After some puppet-master investigation, it was found the three teams that were so far ahead were the internal sales representatives, and they were spending much more time playing the game while at their computers during the day than the outside sales representatives who were only accessing the game on their mobile devices in between sales calls. Realizing that the majority of teams would be upping their game play during the live meeting and not wanting the external sales force to feel they had no chance to win, the points available for each challenge during the national sales meeting were doubled, with the rationale that if the highest scoring teams going into the meeting continued to play well, they would still win; but every team had a chance to catch up at the national sales meeting. In the final scoring, only one of the top three teams before the meeting placed in the overall top three (and that team finished third).

Feedback expressed by learners playing the game, as well as company management, highlighted the benefits of the experience. Learners thought the game challenges "felt real" and represented exactly what they faced in the field. The salesforce asked to continue the training with the characters ongoing for future learning initiatives. Participation in the game was voluntary, but about 84 percent of the salesforce participated in the ARG. The overall response indicated that the ARG was an effective training tool and that the use of ARGs should be supported in future training programs.

NON-PLAYER CHARACTER FACEBOOK PAGE

What started out as one-way communication became a conversation, and this expanded the puppet master's role in the ARG.

Graphic courtesy of Tandem Learning, a division of Ayogo Games.

CASE STUDY: EXTREME MAKEOVER: GRAINGER EDITION

When Grainger, Inc. decided to redesign their website from the ground up, they knew that they would need to train their customer service agents (CSAs) and sales staff on the new functionality and changes in layout so that they could continue to provide excellent customer service. They wanted staff to have experience working with the new website, as well as experience solving potential problems that customers might have. To meet these needs, a scenario-based ARG was designed to highlight each of the major changes to functionality.

Extreme Makeover: Grainger Edition was based within an online portal; however, instead of using meaningless clue codes to gate access to content within the portal itself, or embedding clue codes within website or event content, it required players to solve customer problems and retrieve specific pieces of content from the website to score points. In other words, the clue codes were meaningful answers to customer problems. This design allowed the game to more closely mimic reality, and gave the players a feeling of actually interacting with real customers.

Players accessed customer emails and voicemails within the game portal, which asked for help with specific problems they needed to solve using the new Grainger. com. A typical customer email might ask for help finding compatible parts for an engine that had been previously purchased. The players could find the previous order and look up the required compatible parts for the customer. To show that they had done what was asked, they entered the total price of the parts into the web portal.

Another important piece that allowed the game to exercise more real-world skills was the inclusion of a coaching character. This character, Josh Winter, was introduced to the players as the Grainger district manager of Internet sales. He had a company email address, a profile page within the game portal, and was introduced through a video by two characters that Grainger employees had seen in companywide communication in the past. He sent out instructional emails to the entire group, including bonus clue opportunities, as well as provided some guiding text for each customer communication. A puppet master from outside Grainger then responded to emails sent to Josh, and posted information within the portal using his profile.

Even though he was represented by an illustration, players clearly believed that Josh Winter was an actual Grainger employee. This belief in Josh led to some interesting player interactions over the course of the game. Members of the development team were asked often who "that Josh guy" was, and were greeted with incredulity when they explained that he was a fictional character created for the game. Some players asked Josh questions that only another Grainger employee could answer, and some even responded to him with clear frustration when he was unable to immediately help with issues that were internal to Grainger.

However, despite the fact that players were teamed up to provide game support for each other, players went to Josh for help before using their team messaging area to contact teammates to solve problems. Teams seemed to use the messaging areas primarily to cheer themselves on, and to encourage their teammates to answer more of the scenarios. This was especially strange because there were individual and team winners, so most teams wished to score highly. The most active teams were extremely competitive, and their in-team communication showed that their primary motivation for playing was to win the game.

This was the first time that Grainger had used this style of immersive training. Players were initially hesitant to engage with the game, as it was so different from sitting in a training class and passing a post-test. The time commitment was about equal to the time they would have spent in classroom training, but the idea that they needed to log into the portal each day and work on some short puzzles was a new concept for some of the players. However, after playing, the players really enjoyed that the game allowed them to try things out and explore the new website before it went live. When asked if they felt prepared to help customers with the new functionality, they were confident in their knowledge and said it was the most prepared they had ever felt for a new software launch. In the end, this is the best measure of learning: they felt confident, prepared, and ready to face whatever customer questions arose with the website launch.

EXTREME MAKEOVER COACHING CHARACTER

Players believed he was an actual employee, and they interacted with him for help.

Graphic courtesy of Tandem Learning, a division of Ayogo Games.

10.
PERSONAL BEHAVIOR CHANGE

It's a feature (not a bug) that our brains place inordinate value on things directly in front of us, or short-term payoffs, compared to how we value long-term benefits or consequences. We also have a difficult time placing value on single instances of behavior that only have negative consequences long-term and in aggregate. Michael Fergusson, CEO of Ayogo Games, describes this as the "one cup of coffee rule." For people who need to monitor their sugar intake, like diabetics, putting sugar in your coffee is a no-no. Yet, many still put sugar in their coffee. If they know that putting sugar in their coffee is bad for them, why do they still do it? Because putting sugar in one cup of coffee is meaningless in the grand scheme of someone's health. If you tell someone that putting sugar in the coffee cup in front of them is bad for their health, they could rightfully tell you, "No, it's not." It's the aggregate impact of putting sugar in every cup of coffee that is the problem, not each individual cup of coffee.

The same holds true for organizational issues. Often it is not a single action or decision that negatively affects outcomes, but is the aggregate impact of actions and decisions over time that drives success or failure. When small missteps or incorrect choices compound over time, organizations may find themselves pushing learners to change daily behaviors for which they see no immediate negative consequences and are therefore not motivated to change.

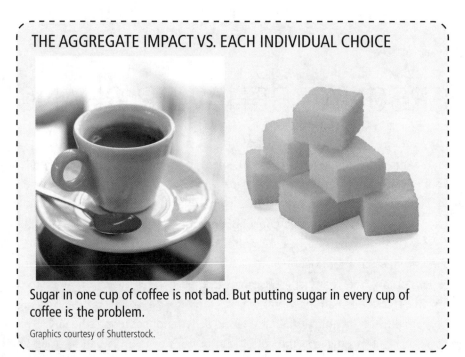

THE AGGREGATE IMPACT VS. EACH INDIVIDUAL CHOICE

Sugar in one cup of coffee is not bad. But putting sugar in every cup of coffee is the problem.

Graphics courtesy of Shutterstock.

IMMERSIVE LEARNING SOLUTION

The challenge for changing personal behaviors is to solve the "one cup of coffee rule" by creating value associated with each cup of coffee, or action. Games are an amazing mechanism for assigning value for each action or decision, as the game can assign extrinsic rewards for each behavior until the intrinsic reward of the long-term aggregate of behaviors can be appreciated by learners. By rewarding the specific instances of good decision making, games can establish behavioral patterns or habits that are more strongly reinforced in combination with the long-term positive benefits that accompany these patterns of positive behaviors.

Immersive learning can not only provide a way for assigning meaning to incremental behaviors to establish new behavioral patterns, but it can also provide insight into larger performance contexts. Sometimes an individual's decisions or behaviors make sense within their limited scope of vision, but when viewed within the bigger picture of organizational goals, individual actions take on greater importance and meaning, or have much farther reaching implications. Immersive learning can provide these views and perspectives that help learners see their individual piece and how it fits within and affects the organizational puzzle.

CASE STUDY: THE CHANGE GAME

In chapter 4, *The Change Game* was discussed as an example of a 3-D immersive game that allows learners to reflect on how they respond to change in order to reduce resistance. It was originally designed for a car company struggling during the lagging economy to get employees at the dealership level to implement changes as they were communicated down from the corporate offices. The problem was that each dealership was run independently, but was governed by corporate office policies that the corporate offices had no power to enforce. The result was that while companywide policies were set at the corporate level to adjust to volatile market conditions, the dealerships were often noncompliant and created serious financial strain across the company.

In looking at the problem, one solution was to address resistance to change on the individual employee level. If each employee understood his own resistance to the changes being implemented and what was driving that resistance, then the awareness would help him be more resilient and adaptable to change. The first challenge was to find content that was appropriate to tackle this specific challenge; that content was found in the work of the Resilience Alliance organization and from one of the authors of *Managing Change With Personal Resilience*, Dr. Linda Hoopes. Dr. Hoopes works with organizations on building resilience as a change management strategy and details seven factors of personal resilience that served as the basis of the game.

THE CHANGE GAME EXAMPLE

Characters in *The Change Game* exhibited resilience factors, and the ship succeeded or failed based on players' identification of those factors.

Graphic courtesy of Tandem Learning and Linda Hoopes.

To create a story line and theme that was accessible across a broad audience, a spaceship theme was selected. The basic story line focused on a new captain being assigned to an existing spaceship and crew and implementing new policies that changed how the crew was used to working. Because of the personal nature of the content, the game was designed as an observational game, with learners watching characters interacting in response to decisions made by the captain. Learners watched the characters exhibit resistance in failure of one of the seven factors of personal resilience. After watching the character scenarios, players were asked to identify which of the seven resilience factors the learner was not exhibiting. If the learner answered correctly, the ship stayed on course, but if not, it veered off course toward an asteroid belt. If three scenarios were incorrectly identified, the ship crashed into the asteroid belt and the learner had to start again.

After each scenario, learners were asked to reflect on a time they faced a similar challenge to the characters in the game and to describe how resilient to the change they were. Because the goal of the game is to encourage open self-reflection in the context of learning about the factors of personal resilience, two versions of the game were created. The first was a "practice" version where learners knew that their scores were not used for tracking performance; the second was an assessment version that learners would complete when they thought they were ready to officially apply their knowledge. In the assessment version, reflections and self-assessments, in addition to the game score, were compiled for the employee's manager to review to facilitate coaching.

Unfortunately, the process of developing this game required its own type of resilience: Just as the development of the game was beginning, the car company that originally wanted the game laid off a significant portion of its corporate office staff, including the project initiator, and the project was cancelled. Undeterred, Tandem Learning and Resilience Alliance approached a pharmaceutical client who was undergoing major internal changes and who had contracted with the Resilience Alliance to provide consulting services for their leadership development. The company agreed to fund the development of the game, as the content related to their internal challenges and had been designed to be context agnostic.

Delivered in conjunction with consulting focused on personal resilience in response to organizational change, *The Change Game* was rolled out to global employee teams to help them build a common vocabulary with managers on how each person's resilience was supporting—or in some cases resisting—change. The pharmaceutical company saw much greater communication among employee teams as a result of the game, and managers were able to better coach employees on specific resilience challenges to make changes happening across the company less disruptive.

THE CHANGE GAME EXAMPLE 2

Since the situation in the game was not as realistic, players could self-reflect and not take any issues personally.

Graphic courtesy of Tandem Learning and Linda Hoopes.

CASE STUDY: HEALTHSEEKER

Millions of people have diabetes and most of them know what they should be doing in regard to diet and exercise, but a shockingly low percentage of patients (7 percent) are actually adherent to these guidelines (Joslin Diabetes Center, 2009). What better strategy than a game to increase patient adherence by providing extrinsic motivation?

Healthseeker is the world's first-of-its-kind game on Facebook. It was developed by Ayogo in collaboration with the Diabetes Hands Foundation (DHF) and the Joslin Diabetes Center (Harvard Medical School), and was funded by Boeringher Ingleheim Pharmaceuticals Inc. (BIPI). *Healthseeker* was designed to motivate better lifestyle choices by people living with diabetes, so that they improve both their nutritional and physical health.

By using a game design approach that will be familiar to players of popular casual social games, *Healthseeker* uses achievements, virtual prizes, and gifting to create instant rewards for healthy behavior, bridging the gap between intentions and action. As action steps are completed in real life and players return to report their progress, they receive experience points and other instant awards for their achievements. Badges and experience points accumulate over time and help the player advance to different levels. Special virtual pats-on-the-back called "kudos" can also be collected, but can only be given away to other players as a show of support. Players can also record their progress and thoughts about their day on their Fridge Door, a wall that displays supportive and inspirational messages from anyone playing the game. The game utilizes the player's own social graph and uses their friends as sources of inspiration and support as they push beyond intention to live their actions.

There are goals, missions, and simple action steps players complete to help them get started on the road to better health. The first step is to review a list of goals the game provides and identify the ones they would like to achieve by playing. Then, they choose from a list of possible missions that are designed to help complete their goals. Once they select a mission that looks challenging as well as fun, they must choose three specific, but simple, action steps from a menu to complete the mission. The action steps are activities players can do on their own or with family and friends. These activities can also be easily incorporated into everyday life. As a player completes action steps and returns to the game to report their achievements, they receive experience points. Each mission has four to five levels. The game becomes more ambitious as a player completes each level. Players are rewarded for their achievements with points that can be used to obtain badges or trophies, and by receiving kudos from their friends.

Healthseeker also uses multiple social media tools to help players and their friends keep each other motivated. Players can challenge each other to complete a mission (for which both receive extra points), give kudos for achievements, and invite others to join them.

Effectiveness can be measured by the average number of healthy actions taken in the game, the difference between players who are active users and active social users, and the impact of play styles on player behavior in the real world related to diet and exercise. Since the game launched in June 2010, it has become a viral phenomenon among the online diabetes community, with approximately 7,200 players who have completed more than 32,900 healthy actions and eaten more than 15,900 healthy meals as logged in the game. Players who receive encouragement from their friends in the game have, on average, 2.5 times as many healthy actions as players who don't—this is the power of social connections.

Healthseeker motivates small actions by giving small rewards, and those rewards were designed to leverage what we understand about how our brains work: small amounts of motivation spur small actions in small periods of time for small (virtual) rewards.

In *Healthseeker,* we focused on two things:

- Instant gratification rewards for healthy activity, in contrast to the usual approach of making long-term health your reward for doing healthy things.
- Making those instant gratification rewards something that you can use to reward the healthy behavior of other players.

The premise is that these two compulsion loops—one of pattern completion, and one of reciprocal social obligation—would reinforce each other and make the game more effective in producing action.

An interesting example of how "social challenge invitations" motivate behavior, even when they weren't accepted, emerged during game play. When a player chooses a mission, he has the opportunity to challenge a friend to do the mission with him. This feature was included in the game because it was believed it would be more motivating for players if they could involve friends in the challenge. What was unexpected-was that people who received a challenge became highly motivated to complete missions. In *Healthseeker*, the average player has done six healthy missions after the first two months of playing. A player who has sent at least one challenge to a friend has done an average of 12 missions—twice as many. But players who have received a challenge—even if they haven't acknowledged the challenge—have done (on average) three times as many healthy missions; and people who have accepted these challenges have completed slightly more missions. Receiving acknowledgment from another player that she cares about your health enough to include you in her mission was highly motivating to healthy behavior.

11.
WORKING TOGETHER

There are very few situations where people work in isolation; the vast majority of what organizations do requires people to work together. Whenever people work together, challenges arise: communication issues, different viewpoints and interests, different and sometimes conflicting motivations, and disparate drivers of individual versus organizational goals. These issues can be minor distractions that affect productivity, or they can be enormous business issues with far-reaching implications. Addressing the issues that arise from people working together can be complicated, especially as the problems of working together can manifest in various ways.

One pervasive issue when people work together is interpersonal communication. On an individual level, our personal differences can dramatically affect our ability to effectively communicate with others who we are required to interact with as part of our job. Our culture, gender, geographic location, and prior knowledge all affect our interpersonal communication skills. Our motivations and goals do as well. The cliché of communication being a two-way street is also true: Communication is not just talking, but is also listening. Our receptive and expressive communication can both cause issues as we strive to work together. When communication breaks down for any of these reasons, it can affect the success of an organization in many ways. Creating common expectations for interpersonal communication can improve how people interact at all levels and can improve processes and outcomes throughout the organization.

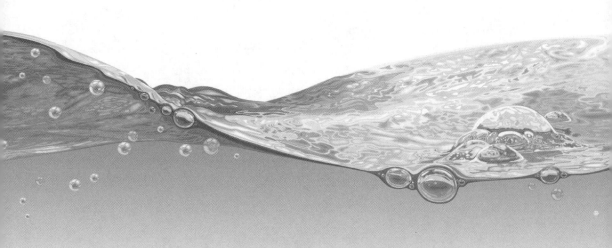

While one-on-one interpersonal communication has dramatic impact on the individual level, how project teams work together and communicate can also be a major organizational issue. When teams work well together, projects are completed more efficiently and effectively and move the organization forward; when teams do not function well, projects may be late, over budget, or the quality is not what was expected. Team success often relies on team communication, but also on following processes that allow each team member to do her job more effectively. Organizations that create skilled and agile project teams are much more likely to succeed where others fail.

Team tasks and processes that must be completed as part of projects or the daily course of work are more ably done with practice. However, it is a challenge to find ways for teams to practice together outside of "real work." Creating opportunities for teams to master tasks or processes in traditional training environments is almost impossible because the context is so critical to team success. Companies that foster collaborative environments—allowing people to work together more effectively synchronously and asynchronously—will have a competitive advantage over organizations that have teams figuring things out as they go, making mistakes along the way.

More and more companies have diversified in terms of geographic location so that workers can be spread all over the globe (Grant Thornton, 2013). This makes communication—and more importantly, collaboration—much more challenging in today's business environment. A small team of individuals can no longer sit around a conference room table and work up business plans, new product designs, or process improvements. Email, conference calls, and web conferencing have filled some of the void, but often they lack the back-and-forth dialogue and direct interaction that once fueled the conference room discussions. Without multi-user document sharing you can't draw diagrams via a conference call as you could do on a whiteboard, and it's impossible to pass around a prototype for inspection.

Additionally, developing employees and leaders is an ongoing struggle for every organization. Once you've invested in hiring someone, every moment they spend on the job is an investment you've made in them, building their knowledge of how to help support your organization's goals. Popular wisdom says that people don't leave companies, they leave bad bosses, which puts additional pressure on leadership development to not only drive the organization forward, but to attract and retain the best talent. As organizations continue to become more geographically dispersed and global, the need for employees to feel connected, coached, and mentored is ever more important. Bringing the right people together to develop employees and leaders is not an easy feat with traditional training structures, and in particular, e-learning courses.

All of these business issues are focused on the challenges created for businesses when people need other people to do their jobs. Most training and learning that addresses these challenges focuses on presenting the steps in the process, or procedural guidelines for people to follow. The real challenge to process and procedure, however, is when people have to follow them in context. Learning experiences that don't provide this practice in context will not prepare teams for the common issues that arise when working together, and will not help individuals learn how to communicate with others more effectively.

IMMERSIVE LEARNING SOLUTION

Immersive learning provides opportunities for people to work together in context. While individual problem solving and complex decision making is important, the truth is that most problems aren't solved by an individual and most decisions aren't made by one person. The following immersive design strategies can be employed to allow people to practice working with people, making mistakes in training so they are prepared to work together more successfully when charged with real-world challenges. These several strategies will be presented with examples, before the case study at the end.

ROLE PLAY

ROLE-PLAY OPTION 1

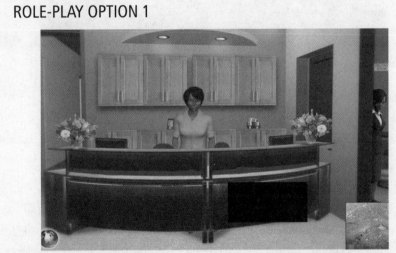

Employees in assistant-type roles can also learn from interactions in the game.

Graphic courtesy of Tandem Learning, a division of Ayogo Games.

Role play within a virtual world or multiplayer 3-D environment is a perfect example of immersive learning. Two or more individuals play specific roles and, unlike a game, there are no winners or losers in role playing. Instead, individuals merely interact with one another in the scenario that they are given. For instance, one role-play scenario may have an individual playing the role of a doctor and another playing the role of a patient in a virtual exam room. In this instance, a new resident may practice clinical skills and the "patient" may be a senior doctor who answers questions as if she were a patient, while observing the resident to provide relevant feedback on the interaction. Through this role-play exercise, the resident may learn more about examining patients and asking appropriate clinical questions through both the interactive experience and from receiving helpful feedback from the senior physician. They play specific roles, and through their role play the resident can learn clinical skills necessary for practicing medicine in the real world without causing any potential harm or stress to actual patients.

ROLE-PLAY OPTION 2

Employees can learn about processes from interactions in the game.

Graphic courtesy of Tandem Learning, a division of Ayogo Games..

In business, companies often use role-play exercises to train staff on different scenarios that they may encounter in their day-to-day work experiences. For instance, the company may have one employee play the role of a customer and the other play the role of a salesperson trying to sell a new product to that customer. Through this interaction both employees get better insight into their customers' perspective as well as learn new techniques to sell products to those customers. In the military, a similar approach was used by the ATEC team to design a training environment that teaches personnel about cultural issues when interacting with people in Afghanistan and Iraq. Called

"First Person Cultural Trainer," the virtual environment allows soldiers to interact with community members and provide verbal and nonverbal cues to indicate whether the player is interacting favorably or unfavorably (Markham, 2010).

Role play is a valuable learning tool when it can be implemented effectively. However, traditional role play has some limitations. Role play requires that individuals are present in the same location. Also, it is unlikely that the environment for the role play will simulate an environment where the actual experience would take place. As a result, it could be distracting for the participants or they may not be able to fully engage in their roles because of their surroundings.

Immersive role playing overcomes the limitations of the real world. It places the participants in a virtual environment that can mirror the equivalent real-world environment. For example, if the real interaction would take part in an office, the role-play activity can take place in a virtual office; if it is a warehouse, then a virtual warehouse, and so on. Furthermore, the use of 3-D learning environments, virtual worlds, or multiplayer games allows users from any location to take part in the role play. A company could have trainers located at their corporate headquarters involved in role-play exercises with employees located throughout the world, without any need for individuals to travel.

ROLE-PLAY OPTION 3

Employees can learn from fantastic game story lines as well.

Graphic courtesy of Tandem Learning, a division of Ayogo Games.

To help better illustrate how role playing can take place within a virtual environment, let's examine a scenario wherein a potential job candidate practices interviewing for a job. The job candidate in this case may have very little experience with interviews. He may be worried about interviewing for a professional position and how he'll perform under the pressure of a real interview. As he doesn't want to go to an interview unprepared, he decides to seek some assistance through a virtual world interview center. This would allow him to role play an interview with an interviewing specialist who could then provide coaching and feedback on his interview skills. Again, this candidate and the interview specialist with whom he interacts could be located anywhere.

Scheduled for an interview, the candidate would arrive for the interview with his avatar dressed appropriately. The candidate would then be interviewed as if he was attending a real job interview. The career center would be structured to resemble a real-world office so the candidate could get the sense of what it would be like to sit in a manager's office or a conference room and run through an entire interview. The interview could be recorded and a career counselor could then review the interview, provide coaching feedback in writing, or conduct a debrief session with the candidate. The candidate could do all of this from his own home, gaining valuable interview experience and feedback as a result of the virtual role play. Given that candidates typically only have one opportunity to "get it right" in an interview, practicing the interviewing process allows candidates to improve in a risk-free environment, therefore minimizing mistakes in a real interview.

In this scenario, the virtual role-play activity takes place around a candidate seeking a job, but nearly any interaction between two or more people could be conducted as a role play within a virtual environment, including sales calls and other customer interactions, job-specific skills training, management training, and so on. The opportunity of role play to improve performance without needing participants and coaches to be in the same physical space gives virtual environments an advantage over live role play in both time and travel costs. Role play in a virtual environment enables real-time interaction and feedback in an immersive environment that can more closely resemble a real-life interaction than many face-to-face role plays allow.

COACHING

One growing area of immersive coaching is in sports. The Coaches Centre launched in 2011 is one example of an immersive environment where athletes, coaches, and other sports professionals can connect online with a goal of encouraging collaboration and performance improvement for athletes (The Coaches Centre, 2012). Businesses want to pass along their expertise and knowledge from senior staff to newly hired staff to bring the new employees up to speed in product knowledge, company policies and practices, processes, customers, and so on. Often a company will assign coaches or mentors (for example, a more experienced staff member) to work with new employees to teach them all of the necessary information to function within their new positions and to ensure that knowledge is spread across the organization. Similarly, employees with expertise in a particular area may be asked to provide training sessions to other staff on those particular areas of expertise, again with the intent of increasing overall knowledge within the organization and decentralizing the knowledge base within the company.

VIRTUAL COACHING EXAMPLE

In VenueGen, coaching can take place in many environments, such as medical centers, office environments, courtrooms, or banks.

Graphic courtesy of VenueGen.

In a traditional, single-office business this can work well. However, as brick and mortar businesses have evolved, traditional coaching practices are more difficult to implement. Increasing numbers of employees work remotely and are therefore not in the office to interact with one another, or they travel and are not in the office for long stretches of time. More and more companies have offices spread across the country or around the globe, and specific expertise may not be available in every location. As a result, it is difficult to get appropriate staff members together to provide coaching and training beyond very limited prescheduled sessions. Companies may try to compensate for this by having coaching take place via email or telephone conversations. With email, there can be considerable delays in exchanging information and it can take days to resolve miscommunications. Conference calls, video conferencing, and web meetings may work better because they occur in real time, but it is often difficult for senior staff members to give contextualized feedback or to fully engage the new hire in the learning process. As a result, there may be good dialogue, but the coaching may be incomplete.

Immersive learning environments can help to recapture the traditional coaching approach by allowing employees to come together within the virtual environment for coaching or mentoring regardless of where the coach and the trainee happen to be located. Let's review a few simple, contextualized examples to illustrate the value that virtual environments bring to the coaching process.

A German engineering company decides to open an office in New York to gain U.S. market share. They open the office and make several new hires. For a brief period of time, the German company decides to have a limited number of its German staff work out of the U.S. office to get the American new hires up to speed on company policies, procedures, and practices. After some time, these employees return to Germany. The newly formed U.S. team is on its own. While the German and U.S. employees could trade emails or conference calls, there are either delays associated with coaching using this approach (particularly given the difference in time zones), or it is difficult for the German staff to show the U.S. staff how to do anything. Video conferencing can solve some issues, but there are difficulties scheduling appropriate times for both teams and the video conferences are not as helpful with role plays or procedural practice. As a result, nearly everything is discussed and described in writing, making the learning process more cumbersome and opening up more opportunities for miscommunication, misunderstanding, and disconnects between the U.S. and German team members. Overall, the German team members don't have the opportunity to show their U.S. counterparts how to accomplish tasks; they are limited to only being able to tell them what to do.

The coaching process could be tremendously improved by using a virtual environment. The German and U.S. staff members could both access the virtual environment to have real-time discussions. As an added benefit, the German team would be able to show the U.S. employees how to accomplish various tasks by performing them in the virtual environment with their avatars. The U.S. team members could see demonstrations of tasks by the experienced German employees and could perform tasks, allowing the German coaches to evaluate their performance and provide real-time feedback.

In addition, as the U.S. office continues to grow, it is unlikely that the German office would regularly be able to assign coaches on site for new U.S. staff. However, with the use of a virtual environment, the German staff could continue to act as coaches or mentors for new hire U.S.-based staff.

As another example, consider a salesforce spread across the country. The sales manager has considerable experience and could certainly provide coaching and mentoring to the sales team; however, given that none of the sales team is located in the same geographic area, the majority of the time the sales manager can only provide coaching over the phone or via email. If the sales manager wants to hold group coaching sessions, the only tools that really work are teleconferences or webinars—primarily one-way communication, with limited opportunity for the group to truly engage with each other or the sales manager.

Within a virtual environment, the sales manager could hold coaching sessions for the sales team at the same time, perhaps in a virtual auditorium. The sales manager could give a presentation, take questions from the group, demonstrate scenarios to the group and have members of the sales team interact with each other. The sales manager could hold individual role-play sessions with sales representatives where the sales manager plays the role of a customer and the sales reps need to try to "sell" him particular products. The sales manager could provide direct feedback to the sales reps immediately following the virtual sales interaction.

Collaboration is about people knowing enough about each other, what they like to work on, what their style of leadership looks like, what they are passionate about—in short, knowing people in ways that go well past what's on someone's résumé. It's also about being able to work effectively together once teams are formed, so coordination can be part of collaboration.

Virtual environments have opened an entirely new avenue for businesses to return to core collaboration by essentially allowing employees, regardless of their location, to meet and share thoughts and ideas to work together. Virtual worlds have the potential to not only revive the traditional conference room discussions, but also to bring in new capabilities to enhance these meetings in ways that weren't possible in the past. For example, an engineer could present multiple designs or virtual 3-D prototypes for a new product that could be inspected and discussed as in a traditional environment. Then additionally, he could incorporate some of the feedback as it is being discussed and make immediate changes. Other engineers could make modifications to the prototypes themselves to better illustrate their proposed enhancements during the course of the meeting. And ultimately, when the meeting was over, an actual prototype that includes all of the changes approved during the meeting would be instantly available. Virtual environments can easily bring about this type of collaboration, and can do so in a way that can expedite development while at the same time saving costs that would normally be associated with creating real-world prototypes. This is just one example of the type of enhanced collaboration that immersive environments can offer.

VIRTUAL MEETINGS

As a basic starting point for immersive collaboration, let's look at virtual meetings. You may not think of meetings as learning environments, but consider this: Meetings are the main point of contact for many employees in organizations. Meetings are where ideas are shared, processes are defined, and decisions are made. Meetings are where we have the biggest opportunity to express ourselves, promote our opinions, present relevant information, and facilitate change. Meetings, in many organizations, are the primary training and learning environment. In that context, it is important to examine how immersive design can influence the effectiveness and success of meetings. As noted previously, it is not uncommon for companies to have employees spread over large geographic areas. Even in cases where employees are predominantly local, it is not uncommon for some employees to work from home or be off site conducting business. Thus, organizations are faced with several options in a real-world environment: try to get as many people to one location as possible, try to get everyone on to a conference call or online meeting, or try to provide some combination of these options. The first option may work if everyone is local but increasingly, with the possible exception of small companies, this is not generally the case. As a result, companies must try to get whomever they can on site for the meeting. This may mean expensive travel costs, lost productivity for travel time, or some critical employees that cannot be involved in the meetings because they cannot be on site at a designated time. Essentially this means that companies are paying high costs (in time and money) to conduct meetings that may not have all of the key players involved. Some businesses try to compensate by conducting business discussions on conference calls or via online meetings. Everyone can be involved in the discussion, but how engaged are they? One value of live meetings is the physical presence of attendees, which necessitates a certain level of participation. Activities like writing on whiteboards, brainstorming, and discussions—while able to be conducted over the phone or in a web meeting—require participation to be effective. Without a physical presence, people can more easily disengage.

Virtual environments can help to overcome these obstacles. Imagine a conference room where every individual who needs to take part in a meeting is present even on short notice. No one is late for the meeting because of snowstorms, cancelled flights, or missed connections. It didn't cost any money for attendees to travel to the meeting and they didn't lose any time (or luggage) traveling to attend. On the walls are whiteboards and video screens so that diagrams can be created, displayed, and modified throughout the meeting, and videos can be shown at any time. Audio can be played and outside information can be pulled at any time it is needed. These are just some of the advantages virtual environments have to offer as a meeting space.

Beyond the cost and time savings, the enhanced ability to interact, and the flexibility in scheduling meetings afforded by the use of virtual environments, there are other advantages inherent in using virtual world technology to conduct virtual meetings. For example, it could be a recruiting advantage because the use of such technology would allow a company to hire employees from anywhere in the world and still make them a part of day-to-day operations within the organization. In addition, it could be used to better engage employees. Often employees are hesitant to take part in meetings for various reasons. By conducting meetings in a virtual world, employees may be more likely to interact because they feel their avatar gives them some level of freedom (for example, they may feel that their avatar is speaking up in the meeting, which provides them some level of anonymity). Some employees may find the virtual space more stimulating as a creative environment where they can do or say much more than they do in a real-world meeting.

IBM conducts many of their meetings within a virtual world. They do so globally without having high costs to bring staff together in a single location. And they allow staff of different levels from around the globe to interact in virtual meetings with one another, because the virtual space puts them all on the same plane. A senior staff member with 25 years or more of experience at IBM may have lots of business experience but may have only limited virtual world experience, whereas a new hire may not bring much business experience to the meeting but may bring lots of virtual-world knowledge. By putting these individuals together in a virtual meeting, it is easy to see why collaboration can take place, as each side has something to offer to the meeting. As Chuck Hamilton, director of IBM's Center for Advanced Learning, noted in *Fast Company*, "We're seeing very senior IBMers swimming and flying next to people who have been in the business 10 months. The only thing I can tell you is, they seem pleased to be meeting this way" (Fast Company Staff, 2007). Would this collaboration take place outside of a virtual world? Possibly, but the collaboration would certainly not take place in the way that virtual meetings and interactions allow.

CASE STUDY: I-95 COALITION

When emergency services and first responders need training, it can be expensive and time consuming. Due to the nature of these jobs, much of the training needs to be as realistic as possible so that trainees, when faced with a real emergency incident, can handle their tasks quickly and efficiently. This style of training is not only expensive to run, but often requires trainees to travel long distances to facilities which are set up specifically for this sort of scenario-based emergency training.

The Center for Advanced Transportation Technology Laboratory (CATT Lab) at the University of Maryland and the I-95 Corridor Coalition have partnered to create this sort of realistic training for first responders in a virtual space. Not only does this allow training to go out to a broader audience more efficiently, but the program also now allows different incident management organizations to work and train together.

The 3-D virtual environment allows up to 500 individuals to simultaneously participate in real-time, scenario-based incident management training over the Internet. These individuals can take on different roles to help solve problems they encounter within the environment. They can play as members of the fire, police, EMT, and traffic control teams, or as bystanders and victims. Trainers may play the victims and bystanders to add an extra level of realism to the scenarios, allowing the participants to practice interacting with civilians. The scenarios encompass a wide range of potential incidents, from car fires that cause secondary explosions that could injure emergency services staff and bystanders, to accidents that cause highway shutdowns. To solve the scenarios, the simulation allows participants to interact with items in the environment, such as traffic cones, medevac helicopters, victims, and the accidents.

I-95 COALITION EXAMPLE

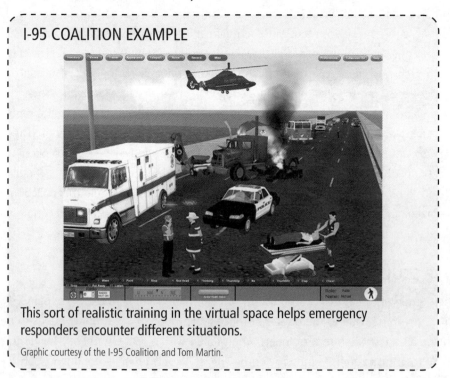

This sort of realistic training in the virtual space helps emergency responders encounter different situations.

Graphic courtesy of the I-95 Coalition and Tom Martin.

Participants also may speak to other participants within the scenario. They may verbally summon help, issue instructions, and speak with other emergency staff, victims, and bystanders to determine the correct course of action. This allows different groups to learn to work together more easily to quickly contain and clear traffic incidents within the I-95 corridor, increasing interagency cooperation and communication. This also could allow agencies to work together to find new and innovative ways to handle emergency situations.

This program not only allows first responder groups to more easily and efficiently train their teams, but it also allows them to test and disseminate best practices and new strategies for incident management. This will result in more educated first responder teams who are aware of the newest and best strategies for handling a particular situation, which will allow for better and safer resolution of highway incidents.

12.
BUILDING SOMETHING BETTER

In the broadest sense, organizations all have a product they are trying to sell, whether it's education, consulting, a process, or an actual product. Each organization strives to create value that is better than the competitor's value – whether that value is perceived or real. In order to be better, organizations typically focus on quality, cost, or speed to differentiate themselves from their competitors, although all three factors must enter into the value equation.

It is the combination of quality, cost, and speed that ultimately determine an organization's value. It is in improving quality, cost, and time to market that immersive design can help organizations excel.

Product quality can be affected by many factors, including quality of design, quality of materials, quality of craftsmanship or skill in development, or quality of user experience. All of these aspects ultimately affect an organization's brand image in the market and affect the success of any particular product in solving customer problems or addressing a market need.

Cost is another important consideration for organizations in how they position themselves in the market. Don't assume that lower cost is always better; in many markets, the lowest cost items are viewed as inferior and customers are willing to pay higher prices for perceived higher quality or first-to-market innovation. Market price is also different from cost of goods sold (COGS); while price should be higher than COGS

in order for an organization to make a profit, the margin between cost and price may vary dramatically and is influenced by quality and speed factors.

Time to market is the third facet of value that organizations should consider for their products. First to market companies may be able to charge a premium, but may run the risk of being ahead of the market in terms of customer needs. Trendsetting companies need to balance their quality and cost to offset that they may have a smaller customer base initially until new products are "proven" and attract a broader audience.

IMMERSIVE LEARNING SOLUTION

In looking at how an organization can improve their quality, cost, and time to market, process and development are two main areas of focus. Immersive learning can help organizations improve their processes and products in ways not previously possible by providing virtual "testing" environments to try out new ideas and see the short- and long-term impacts of changes to processes and products in realistic environments.

PROCESS COLLABORATION

Immersive learning environments can be useful for conducting meetings and can be effective environments in which to share assets like traditional documents or virtual objects. Just as with meetings and document sharing, immersive learning environments can provide ideal conditions for process collaboration.

Once again, let's look at an example of the traditional conference room meeting. A bunch of folks crowd the room (assuming they can all get to the same spot at the same time) and gather around a whiteboard where someone starts to draw a diagram with boxes and interconnecting lines to simulate a process as it exists today. Then someone else suggests changes and boxes are erased or added, new lines are drawn and redrawn, and pretty soon there is a jumble of lines, boxes, and who knows what that tries to best simulate a process in the real world. Sure there is collaboration, but the end result is just a diagram that gets copied down and real-world processes are then (hopefully) changed to try to mimic what is seen in that diagram. Maybe it works and maybe it doesn't. And if it doesn't, then you could repeat the process, trying to erase more lines or add more lines or make an even bigger spiderweb out of the whole process flow. Everyone has seen flowcharts or process diagrams, but there are some people who never quite understand them, as some boxes on paper just don't seem to translate into an actual process for some people. When all is said and done, there currently exists a passable process for developing new or redesigning existing processes.

Why settle for passable? Using immersive environments for process collaboration offers so much more for businesses. As with document sharing, individuals involved in process design are no longer constrained by traditional limitations (so they are no longer tied to flowcharts and diagrams to detail their processes). Instead, a business could quickly create all the physical components of the process in a virtual environment and then be able to have members of its team add or remove various components, easily visualizing the end results of those changes. This would allow companies to experiment with changes—even complex ones—that would not normally be possible (or could be possible but would be more difficult to visualize) in more traditional process design or redesign.

For example, we can look at a small distribution business. As a current process, one individual in the company may receive a phone order and pass it on to another individual to have them create a packing sheet. Once this packing sheet is created it may be delivered to one or more different individuals in a warehouse who would then pull all the items and give them to yet another person to have them package up the items and provide quality control on the order. Finally, the packaged items would then go to a shipping department for distribution out to the customer. This company may determine that it typically takes four hours to complete this process, but they want to reduce that time in half. To improve the turnaround time, the company has many options. They can try automation for some of the steps; they can have certain individuals take responsibility for performing more than one step in the process; they can try to physically relocate staff within their building to eliminate delays in handoffs between these individuals, and so on.

In a real-world process design session, the company may know how long it takes for each step in the process and may be able to identify bottlenecks where the largest delays occur. In turn they could propose some solutions that may or may not lead to process improvements in their environment, and the only way they can then find out if such process changes lead to improvements is to try them out. With so many different variables that can be changed, it can be extremely difficult for a company to choose the right one (or combination of different changes that becomes the right solution). They may have to go through many changes that don't work before they ultimately see any significant improvements.

In a virtual environment, one could create the workflow with avatars, goods, locations, and so on, so that the entire process would unfold for anyone in the company to view. This could be done with minimal cost. And it could be created such that each step is assigned its equivalent real-world time (so that if it takes 20 minutes for a packing sheet to be delivered to the warehouse staff, then 20 minutes could be assigned to this step in the virtual environment). Now the company could try out all the various options available to them without having to make a best guess and deploy them in their real-world environment that would risk causing even larger delays. They could move staff around physically in the virtual world; they could eliminate steps in the process; they could try to add automation to one or more steps; they could allow staff to perform more than one function in the process; and they could measure how each of those changes affected the final overall turnaround time to get the inventory out the door to their customers. Each different step in the process could be modified or steps could be changed in conjunction with one another to try to achieve the best results. Because it is a virtual environment, there is no impact on the actual day-to-day operation of the company until an enhanced process has been designed and tested. This minimizes the overall risk and ultimately has a much smaller cost in the long run, because there is no lost time and revenue associated with a trial and error approach to testing proposed process solutions.

Furthermore, this virtual process design opens up a wider level of collaboration. More individuals can be involved in the process, because there is no risk in making changes in the virtual environment compared to real world process design, which has much greater risk and therefore needs to be controlled more closely. The more individuals involved in the virtual redesign process, the more likely they are to buy in to the final changes to real world process design, because they feel involved in the design of those new processes.

In addition, process collaboration in a virtual environment allows for much more creativity. Things that wouldn't normally be tried in the real world because they would be too costly or too time consuming to try can be developed and implemented in a virtual environment for minimal cost. In this specific company example, it would be possible for the distributor to try out computerized or automated systems to see if these would improve turnaround times. In the real world, these could be expensive mistakes if they made things worse or only provided small improvements in turnaround times. Using the virtual environment would also give the company the opportunity to find out how these systems would be received and utilized by its employees, if they allowed those employees to collaborate in the process design and potentially even try out such systems in a virtual environment.

Virtual process collaboration could even allow the company to determine what pitfalls may occur with the implementation of such systems should that be the selected outcome. These obstacles to implementation could be identified and addressed prior to implementing a new technology or process in the real world company.

PRODUCT DEVELOPMENT

Throughout this chapter the concept of using immersive environments to help improve collaborative processes, development, and testing has been touched upon numerous times. This is an area where immersive environments can provide a huge advantage for companies. Anything that can be done in the real world can be modeled in a virtual environment for marginal time and cost. This means that in very little time products could be developed in a virtual environment for minimal investment. What follows is an example that illustrates how the product development cycle can be greatly enhanced by doing the majority of the development within a virtual environment.

A medical device manufacturer is looking to develop a brand new infusion device to add to its existing product portfolio. Today, this manufacturer would probably follow a process similar to the following.

1. They would go to their product managers and work out specifications for the device based on the experience of the product manager and their history and interactions with the customer base.

2. The manufacturer may also conduct some focus groups or talk with a limited number of its key users to get input on the new device.

3. They may contract with an outside firm to have them conduct market research for the device.

It could easily be several months for all of these data to be assembled, at which point more steps would take place:

4. A set of design criteria and a high level design document would be developed to address all of the necessary features and functionality of the device (for example, will it use standard tubing or a proprietary cassette mechanism, will it have safe drug limit checking or not, what conditions would trigger alarms, what safety measures will be implemented to ensure that the device is designed to reduce medication errors).

5. These features are then discussed in meetings (whether live or via teleconference) and in email messages exchanged to flesh out the specific features that need to be included. Again, there are additional delays associated with this process.

6. Many individuals will need to sign off on what appears to be a final list of approved features and functions.

These features will then be provided to an engineering team who will need to determine how to best implement these features and functions. A human factors team could also be involved to ensure that the design is adequate in terms of human factors, and regulatory affairs could also be involved. They could ensure the necessary design and manufacturing processes are followed and that the device is designed to minimize risk and meet all necessary FDA guidelines.

So there are multiple teams involved at this point working with the design specifications and most likely also still the original team that developed those specifications (so, there are a lot of people involved). All of these groups are working through what components they need to get into the product. As the product design is taking shape, it is continually changing. At each step there are multiple options available and trade-offs for each of those options that must be discussed before final design decisions are made. After more meetings, more discussion, more time, and so on, a final design is drafted and distributed to all the parties involved for another round of approval. By this point many, many months have gone by in the development process.

Let's assume the design is approved. So then the steps begin again.

7. One or more prototypes would be developed, adding more time to the process, and tested in house.

8. Following this round of testing, there would very likely be some adjustments and creation of additional prototypes, adding even more time and cost, and this would continue until a fairly good prototype was available.

9. The prototype would then likely be taken to an advisory board or customer panel to have some actual nurses and doctors try it out and give their feedback. This would be a small sample and based on their feedback, additional changes would be made adding still more time and cost.

10. At this point, the device could just about be finalized and some actual devices could be produced.

A very limited number of alpha test sites, or possibly a first round of alpha sites and then a second round of trials at some beta sites, would be selected and the pumps would be tested at these sites for some time to make sure there weren't any major usability or functionality issues or safety concerns. If none were found, the pump would finally be ready to be rolled out as a new product, assuming FDA approval, of course.

It is easy to see this process could take a year or more to complete at a very significant cost to the company in terms of labor and development. The amount of actual customer feedback that is provided as part of the design process is extremely limited, so much of the design is built around what members of the design team feel would best suit their customers through previous interactions or observations. It's possible that these perceived best features only represent those of a minority user group and don't truly mimic the larger user community. For example, many companies tend to build out their user groups with sites that have advanced users who are looking to push technology to new extremes, whereas the vast majority of customers may never need or use advanced functionality. It may actually make the devices too complex for many users. This design process works as evidenced by the new products launched successfully, but there is a significant cost associated with the process. Worse, there are some products that aren't successful or that require further investment to improve them post-release to make them successful.

Let's look at the design process again, while using virtual environments instead.

1. The company would turn to its product managers, in-house expertise, advisory board, and so on, and determine what would be the best features for the new infusion pump. That part is exactly the same. From this point, however, the process changes dramatically.

2. Because there is not a significant time or cost to build out prototypes or models in a virtual world, product management doesn't necessarily need to spend as much time narrowing down its list of features and functionality.

3. Similarly, engineering doesn't need to spend a lot of time trying to determine the best combination of options to include in the device. Instead, numerous prototypes of the device can be quickly and easily created in a virtual environment. These can include variations in design and functionality to represent numerous product and engineering designs.

4. All of these designs can be tested out by engineering, product managers, and so on within the company worldwide at any time, and feedback can be collected to narrow down the field of proposed features. Again, costs are minimal but the upside is tremendous, because the design can be driven by actual testing of prototypes rather than trying to design on paper or in meetings and coming up with a limited number of designs that can be built in the real world.

5. Furthermore, prototypes can be changed in almost no time as new ideas are generated in the internal virtual testing and development process. As a result, a finalized design could be produced to create a real world prototype in significantly less time while exploring more potential designs and having more individuals involved in the development process—plus on a more global scale.

6. After a virtual prototype is finalized, the company could create a real world prototype to match the final design from the virtual testing. The prototype could be taken out to doctors and nurses as in the real world design example, and significant time and cost savings would already be achieved.

7. But the virtual design process could be taken a step further. Instead of taking a real world prototype to a limited number of clinical staff at customer sites, the company could show the virtual designs to a much larger portion of its customer base. In fact, this could be done earlier in the process. Multiple design ideas could be placed in a virtual environment and customers could be given access to view the prototypes. A much larger population of internal employees, experts, and customers could provide feedback on which designs they prefer or what additional items they'd like to see.

8. Even these changes could be incorporated into the design process before a prototype is ever developed (obviously, the company would need to be protective about divulging ideas that are confidential or could jeopardize the company's business prospects). The company could get broader feedback from around the world and higher quality feedback coming directly from the actual customer base that would be purchasing the product. Perhaps as valuable as collecting feedback, the company

would be engaging that customer base directly in the design process, thereby making the customer feel that their wants and needs are being heard and addressed in the latest infusion pump design. This potentially has the added benefit of making the customer more likely to purchase the product because they know it will meet their needs.

9. Within the immersive environment, the company could set up a virtual hospital that would allow the customer to try out the new pumps on virtual patients in numerous clinical scenarios. This would provide the company with actual product and safety testing in advance of ever having created a single pump in the real world. If, for instance, the company found that one particular feature routinely led to confusion in the virtual hospital, then they could redesign that feature and test it out again in the virtual hospital. This would verify that the proposed changes work, and tie to the overall goal of reducing post-release safety modifications. The final pump design would likely not lead to as many adverse incidents, thereby reducing liability and product costs.

10. It is possible that sometime in the future the FDA or international regulatory bodies may even accept virtual testing as a substitute for real world clinical data to prove the safety and efficacy of medical equipment. Nevertheless, even if this isn't the case, the company could gain valuable clinical data from the virtual hospital scenario. Ultimately, a real world prototype would need to be made and tested in a clinical setting; however, it's likely that this prototype would experience fewer problems, reducing the time needed for prototype testing. The end result would be moving the product to the marketplace quicker, with fewer risks, and fewer costs.

11. Once the product is commercially available, the sales force could then use the virtual hospital as a sales tool to allow clinical staff at hospitals throughout the world to test out the product before they purchase it. Rather than a limited on-site demo to a handful of staff, the virtual hospital could be opened to all staff at a customer site to allow access to try out the product. This virtual hospital would be available anytime so that staff could see the product at their convenience rather than trying to fit in a brief demo of the product between clinical responsibilities, emergencies that arise, other meetings, and so on.

12. Once a hospital purchased the device, the company could use the virtual hospital as another method to provide training to staff. Typically, there are minimal days of on-site training by the vendor. Hospitals often struggle to get all of the staff trained in a timely manner, particularly given the challenges of using per diem staff; having staff cover multiple shifts 24 hours each day; or the constant turnover of staff within healthcare institutions. This topic will be explored in more detail in the next chapter; however, this use and its advantages are worth mentioning here as just another side benefit for using virtual environments for the development of new products.

Through this single example it is evident that product development using virtual environments and virtual prototypes is a significant improvement over traditional, real world product development. Virtual development is less expensive, results in a final product much more rapidly, allows for the exploration of more design features, has the potential to incorporate more customer feedback, and has the ability to better engage customers for future sales of the product, and so on. All of these are enabled through opportunities to practice and refine interpersonal communication, collaboration, coaching, and giving feedback in an authentic context where practicing these skills is complementary to the meaningful work of product prototyping and development. For a small company with limited staff and resources, this is a considerably more attractive option compared to traditional development, but the same could be true for very large companies. Although this example focused on the development of a single medical device, the advantages could translate to any product from any industry for any customer base throughout the world.

13.
DECISION MAKING

Getting information in modern times is easy; the Internet provides us with practically instant access to documents, resources, and people that can answer almost any question and give us whatever information we seek. The real challenge is what to do once we have the information. At the core of behavior change and performance improvement is decision making. Every second of every day, you choose. You decide how long to take a coffee break, what items on your to-do list to prioritize, which job applicant to hire, or which employee to promote. Some decisions are easy; some are complicated with no ideal options. No matter the decision, our minds weigh the pros and cons before deciding. Sometimes it happens instantly: I'll have a vanilla crème because I like it better than the chocolate glazed doughnut. Sometimes people take days, months, and even years to make complex decisions where lots of factors are involved.

In an ideal world, making decisions happens as quickly as possible after considering all of the implications based on all available data. In business, this is particularly important, because decisions made within an organization can affect many people, from employees to stakeholders to customers. Unfortunately, the ideal world rarely exists; decisions sometimes take a long time to make, have lots of people involved in making them, have incomplete information on the implications of various options, or have incomplete data available to base the decision on. Sometimes, we don't even

know what all of the available options are to choose. The more options, implications, and available data, the more complex decision making becomes.

Obviously organizations that have more skilled decision makers are more likely to make better simple decisions, but most importantly, they are likely to make better complex decisions. While some organizations may assess decision-making skills as part of the hiring process, many—if not most—do not. How, then, do you teach or improve decision-making skills within your organization? Not surprisingly, better decision making is part process and part experience. You can train people on the process of analyzing data and weighing options, but much of successful decision making relies on being able to see the potential outcomes of our decisions. That insight comes primarily through experience.

IMMERSIVE LEARNING SOLUTION

The best way to speed up learners' proficiency in making good decisions is to provide them with more opportunities to make decisions and to see the outcomes of those decisions. Even better, letting learners see these outcomes in an immersive learning environment provides the context and experience without the potential risks of making decisions that could affect the organization, customers, or stakeholders. By failing while learning, learners are lowering the likelihood of failing when it counts.

There are all kinds of decision making: for example, financial, social, organizational, or personal to name a few. No matter what type of decision making learners need to practice, when creating an immersive learning environment, it's most important to create the same level of complexity in making the decision as the learner would be faced with in real life. Not only should the complexity be present in the options available and the contributing factors to making one decision over another, but the outcomes and feedback from the decisions, once they are made, should also represent the true range of complex outcomes.

CASE STUDY: GOVERNMENT PROCUREMENT GAME

In chapter 5, you learned about a government agency that needed a learning program to improve procurement decision-making processes within their acquisitions and requirements offices. These employees needed to better understand requirements for putting a contract up for competition and selecting the appropriate contract type. Specifically, they were looking for a game that would allow learners to explore the consequences of different contractual decisions. To meet these requirements, a game was developed that lets learners work through different realistic, narrative-driven contract initiation scenarios and explore the consequences related to decisions they made.

In the game, learners work with a member of the program management team, Kathy—a non-player character—to help her make the acquisitions she needs for her programs. They are coached through the process by another character, Greg, who is the director of the contracting office. The learners are given documents and research to use to make their decisions related to making the contract competitive and which contract type they should pick. At certain times during the game they are also approached by other contracting officer characters for advice on quick questions, which cover some other regulations the learners need to know.

As learners move through the content, their decisions affect the final outcome of their game play; depending on their experience level, they could end up reaching an end result that is less than ideal, losing the game. Once this ending has been reached, players are given the option to start over and make better decisions. In this way, experienced players may avoid pitfalls that new contracting officers may fall into, and they work through the progressively harder scenarios to reach a final, most difficult or "boss-level" type of scenario.

To encourage learners to play the game multiple times—and truly explore the entirety of the content and the consequences they may face for poor decision making—learners are awarded badges and achievements for doing certain things within the game. For instance, a player who loses the game during the first scenario is awarded the "Epic Fail" badge, and one who answers all of the quick questions correctly is awarded a "Trusted Advisor" badge.

A learner who plays through the game without making any mistakes does not collect all of the badges, but can see how many badges they still have to collect. This allows them to go back through the game again and strategically work through the content to collect the rest of the badges. While this may seem like punishment for good behavior, it allows learners to really explore the reasoning behind the regulations and best practices, so that they have a deeper understanding of why a certain decision is the correct one. This will allow new contracting officers to form better relationships with program managers, because they can explain why things need to happen in a certain way.

Throughout the game, learners also need to maintain a good relationship with the program manager (Kathy), and a good reputation within the contracting office. These two measures gate the quick questions and scenario progression, so that learners who do not consciously pay attention to these may find themselves unable to approve contracts over a certain price point or are disliked by Kathy to the point that she will no longer bring her program needs to the learner's character. While these measures are connected to scenario decisions made by the learner, the consequences are not immediate, and mimic similar real-world measures of success. A contracting officer who does not maintain their real-world reputation or program management relationship could sabotage her own career very quickly.

While the game often behaves like a simulation, allowing learners to work through realistic scenarios and see realistic consequences for poor decision making, the emphasis on exploration and collection of endings and achievements pushes players to try things that they might not otherwise try. It shifts the focus from completing a simulation correctly to finding all of the possible ways to lose and win, so that the learners truly understand why they should compete for a contract or choose a fixed price contract.

CASE STUDY: CLINICAL DECISION MAKING WITH VIRTUAL PATIENTS

An ongoing challenge for medical professionals is how to improve clinical decision making for healthcare professionals. It is difficult—if not impossible—to provide consistently varied exposure to patients with whom clinicians can practice their diagnostic skills and treatment decisions. Perhaps more importantly, how do you provide this depth and breadth of experience without patients suffering through the clinician's learning curve?

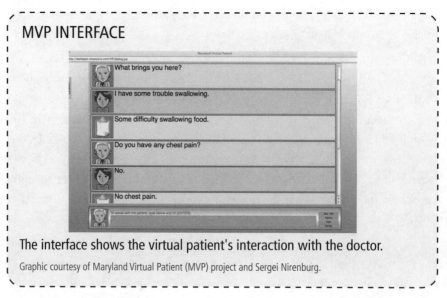

MVP INTERFACE

The interface shows the virtual patient's interaction with the doctor.

Graphic courtesy of Maryland Virtual Patient (MVP) project and Sergei Nirenburg.

MVP UNDER THE HOOD

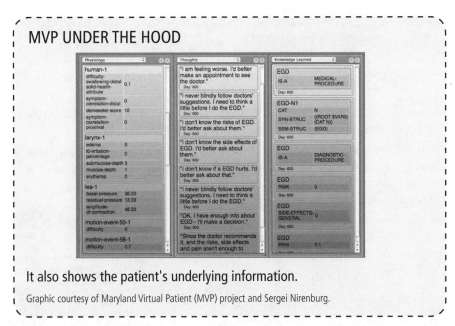

It also shows the patient's underlying information.

Graphic courtesy of Maryland Virtual Patient (MVP) project and Sergei Nirenburg.

MVP AGENT

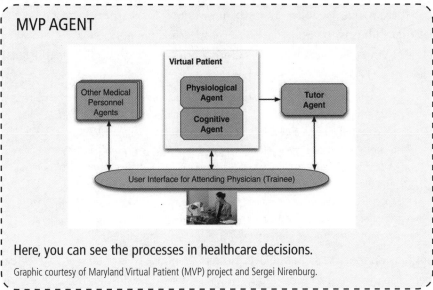

Here, you can see the processes in healthcare decisions.

Graphic courtesy of Maryland Virtual Patient (MVP) project and Sergei Nirenburg.

These challenges were the motivation for the Maryland Virtual Patient (MVP) project.

Their desired outcomes for the project included:

- Trainees should be exposed to a variety of disease categories, including chronic and acute disorders as well as simple and complex diseases.

- Trainees should have access to many patients suffering from each disease, with each patient displaying clinically relevant variations on the theme. Such variations might involve the path or speed of disease progression, the severity of symptoms, responses to treatments, or secondary disorders present that could affect treatment choices.

- Trainees should have the opportunity to independently manage the care of many such patients in a context in which trial and error learning carries no risk.

- User interventions should actually change patient physiology and dynamically affect the future existence of the patient.

- The knowledge substrate should be readily extensible both to new diseases and to newly discovered information about already modeled diseases. It should accommodate both poorly and well-understood knowledge about disease processes.

- The environment should provide a mentoring component that reuses the same knowledge underpinning the simulation and extends it with knowledge of best clinical practices.

- The mentoring should be carried out using natural language.

The MVP project is clearly embracing the potential of immersive learning, and pairing immersive design with elements of artificial intelligence and physiological changes that provide feedback and evolving context for learners in response to their clinical interactions with virtual patients. These virtual patients, or MVPs, are a specialized class of virtual humans who are suffering from a disease or disorder. As McShane et al. describe MVPs:

> A key design feature of MVPs is their automatic autonomous function in response to internal stimuli and external interventions. Responses can be both cognitive and physiologic in nature. A cognitive response is exemplified by the MVPs' capabilities for answering trainees' questions about symptoms, lifestyle, family history, and so on. A physiologic response is exemplified by the change of relevant property values after an intervention like medication or surgery. MVPs show realistic responses both to expected and to unexpected interventions, so if a trainee launches an inappropriate (unexpected) treatment, the MVP's state will not improve and may even deteriorate, in which case the trainee must attempt to recover from his mistake (2013).

Not only do the MVPs change over time in response to stimuli from the clinicians, but their diseases are also modeled to progress over time, just as the disorder or disease might evolve in real life. Scripts for these virtual patients are written by authors and reflect specific trends, patterns, and anomalies that can occur in patients who have a particular disease or disorder.

Clinicians are first introduced to virtual patients of whom they have no prior knowledge. Through a series of interactions that may include questions or diagnostic tests, the clinician attempts to come to a diagnosis. Through deductive reasoning, they eventually diagnose the virtual patient. At any point in the process, the clinician can choose a treatment for the virtual patient. Depending on the treatment selected, the virtual patient will respond positively or negatively based on the virtual patient script and disease model.

This type of truly immersive, automated, and interactive learning environment is an example of current technology's capability to recreate reality, in all of its complexity, for training purposes. Realistic, repetitive, and representative: Immersive environments such as the MVP project have the potential to not only create expertise more quickly, but also to save lives. This kind of learning is effective, as evidenced in the evaluation of another technology-based scenario-driven learning system focused on complex decision making: the SHERLOCK II, which teaches troubleshooting for electronics. In the evaluation of SHERLOCK II, "it was reported that technicians learned more from using this system for 24 hours than from four years of work in the field" (Evens and Michael, 2006). While full-scale simulations may seem costly and time-consuming to design, the cost and benefit of the time it would otherwise take to improve performance and the implications of an extended learning curve should be part of the investment decision to create a comprehensive learning experience like the MVP project.

14.
THE REAL WORLD

No matter how many training scenarios you present or how much someone practices, ultimately, the proof is in performance. Learning doesn't stop when you leave a training environment and need to do what you've been training for; we learn from all of our experiences. How can organizations support learning during performance?

Performance support as a concept has in the past been limited to "job aids" that were usually quick tip cards that someone could keep close at hand as a reminder of critical information. Now, with mobile devices readily accessible and able to convey information anywhere and in context, performance support is taking on new dimensions. Still, what is the best way to support performance? What are the best ways to help people learn in the real world? And how can mobile devices be leveraged to their best advantage?

Organizations are recognizing the shift to a mobile workforce, even in traditionally non-mobile roles. Smartphones are becoming smarter, cheaper, and more accessible as Wi-Fi and 3G signals are available in ever expanding geographical regions. Even with these technologies now being used by students and employees for their everyday activities and communication, organizations are struggling to leverage their powerful capabilities to support performance on demand.

IMMERSIVE LEARNING SOLUTION

Mobile devices and social media are touted as the new generation of performance support tools, but once again, the focus should be on the design—not the tools. For performance support, the ultimate integration of mobile devices and immersive experiences can be seen in augmented reality.

Augmented reality has been defined in many ways, sometimes including QR codes or location-based social media tools. These definitions are too broad and confuse the pure experience of augmented reality: where perception of reality is changed through an augmentation of the environment. To date, the best definition of augmented reality is from Specht et al. (2011), who define augmented reality as "a system that enhances a person's primary senses (vision, aural, and tactile) with virtual or naturally invisible information made visible by digital means." This definition, by focusing on sensory perception, helps differentiate augmented reality from location-based data applications that, while they provide additional contextual data, do not alter your experience of reality nor immerse you in an augmented experience.

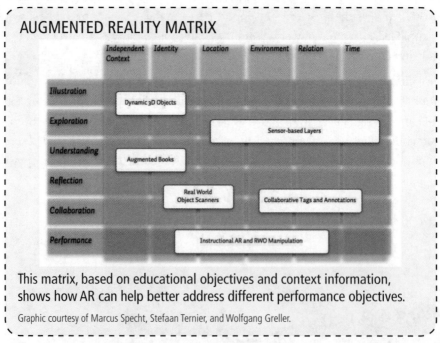

AUGMENTED REALITY MATRIX

This matrix, based on educational objectives and context information, shows how AR can help better address different performance objectives.

Graphic courtesy of Marcus Specht, Stefaan Ternier, and Wolfgang Greller.

While augmented reality is arguably in its infancy, there are an increasing number of examples of how organizations are using augmented reality to help them achieve their goals. From an organizational learning perspective, Specht et al. have created a "Matrix Classifying Educational Patterns for Mobile AR Based on Educational

Objectives and Context Information" to better define how AR can help address different learning and performance objectives.

This graphic demonstrates different levels of AR, from augmented books or texts to instructional AR and virtual manipulation of the real world that is the foundation of immersive performance support.

CASE STUDY: ON-SITE REPAIRS BY MILITARY MECHANICS

No matter how skilled a mechanic may be, he is not infallible. In a critical combat moment or when time is of the essence, providing support information in context could potentially save lives. In a subject-controlled research study by Henderson and Feiner (2009), the efficacy of using a tracked head-worn augmented reality display as a performance support tool under field conditions was examined in comparison to an untracked head-worn display (information that was always within the mechanic's line of sight, but did not change with his visual focus) and a fixed flat-panel display. Eighteen common tasks were performed by the mechanics to gauge how well the tracked augmented reality solution facilitated improvements in performance compared to the other methods.

The results of the study were not shocking. Not only did the tracked, head-worn augmented reality application enable mechanics to locate and perform their tasks more quickly, in some cases the mechanics had less head movement. Not only were the quantitative measures improved, but the mechanics found the AR tracked application more intuitive. They also reported that they found it more satisfying to use than the other methodologies.

While this research study was focused on military mechanics, you can see how augmented reality applications could help with real-time, contextualized performance support for any type of hands-on task. While much technology-enabled learning is focused on white-collar workers, augmented reality is an ideal solution for blue collar performance support. Equipment repair, maintenance, and assembly-line work are just some types of under-served employee populations for whom augmented reality performance support would be ideal.

CASE STUDY: ARIS AND DOW DAY

In October 1967 at the University of Wisconsin–Madison, Dow Chemical arrived on campus to recruit students, and they were greeted by protesters who were opposed to Dow's production of napalm that was being used in the Vietnam War. To learn about this event, you can read all about the violent escalation of those protests, or you can walk to the actual location where the events of those two days took place. But what is another option?

ARIS OVERLAY

You can see historical photographs overlaid onto actual locations.

Graphic courtesy of Aris.

Dow Day—a "situated documentary"—was developed to teach about the historical campus protests at the University of Wisconsin and showcase the unique capabilities of ARIS. ARIS is an open source mobile augmented reality application that allows designers to leverage story, characters, and game mechanics to create an interactive, immersive, geo-located experience. In Dow Day, you play the role of a reporter learning about the events of the Dow Day protests as you travel to different locations around the campus. You interview Dow employees, students, and police, seeing the events of those two days in October 1967 through their eyes. When I say "through their eyes," I mean almost literally; the game uses augmented reality to overlay historical photographs over actual locations to allow you to not only hear about the protests through characters representing those involved, but also to see what it looked like during the protests.

While the previous example of mechanics using augmented reality for performance support was primarily context driven (providing support in context at the time of need), the use of an application like ARIS can allow you to create story line, characters, and contextual decision making. This can provide contextualized training in real-world environments. Imagine learners leveraging a mobile augmented reality training environment as they go about the business of their day, with training scenarios becoming available as they visit different customer locations, or different locations within your organization. This type of design would be ideal for process training: coaching

ARIS VIDEO

You can see historical videos overlaid onto actual locations.

Graphic courtesy of Aris.

learners along the process and challenging them at each step. Additionally, an augmented reality mobile experience with geo-location requirements may make an excellent asynchronous team player design: Completion of an activity relies on team members finishing up different portions of a task in context.

ARIS QUEST

You receive quests that require you to travel to different locations, not unlike a scavenger hunt.

Graphic courtesy of Aris.

SECTION 4

WRAP-UP

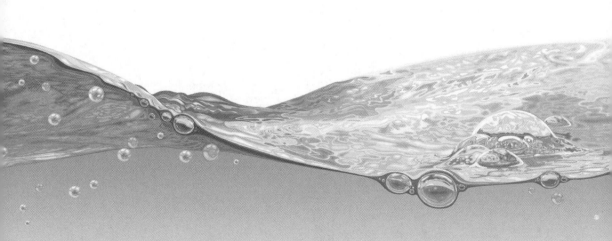

15.
THE FUTURE OF IMMERSIVE LEARNING

PREPARING FOR IMMERSIVE LEARNING

So. What can you do now? The future of learning is mobile, just in time, social, experiential, and driven by analytics. It will still need to be scalable—but increasingly, it will need to be personalized. As we evolve as a technology-driven global economy, our learning experiences will need to evolve too. If our educational and training methodologies don't evolve, they will become obsolete.

Immersive learning as a design concept is the next evolution of training, but don't assume that the need for this transformation of thinking will be readily embraced by organizations. Immersive learning design requires critical analysis of organizational development, application of cognitive theory, and in many cases, utilization of game design skills. How many times do you hear of these skills being valued by the business—or if they are, how often are they encouraged in learning or training?

As discussed earlier, to improve performance, you need to have a deep understanding of all of the factors that together lead to successful performance. Plus, you need to understand that when certain factors are lacking, they negatively affect performance. In essence, you need to understand what it is that makes an organization

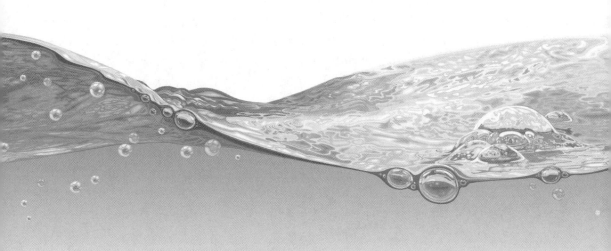

successful and then meticulously create experiences to bring along those members of the organization that are not performing as expected.

As learning professionals, we need to clearly identify and communicate the value of our role in business terms to the rest of the business. We are not simply helping people "learn." We are helping people perform at a higher level to improve organizational performance. All learning and training initiatives should be framed within that context, but it is especially critical for immersive learning. Why? Because immersive learning is not simply knowledge acquisition—it is the application of knowledge and skill in context in a way that can and should be directly tied to key performance metrics. Immersive learning is unique in that it allows people to practice and tracks their performance metrics for that practice, making it easy to answer the question, "How does this learning initiative impact the business?"

Are you ready to get started? Do you know where to start? Follow these steps, and review the appropriate chapters in this book for support as you tackle challenges along the way:

Step 1: Identify the organizational problem to solve. Think in terms of what people need to do differently (not just know or think differently). Create performance objectives, not learning objectives. Focus your objectives; too big and you may never get your project off the ground, too small and you may not create enough complexity to allow for varied practice.

Step 2: Analyze. Poke holes in your hypotheses and be ready to be wrong or surprised by what you uncover. Talk to people: stakeholders, learners, customers, managers. Make sure you understand the problem from all sides. Look for the metrics and measure the current state. Set benchmarks for success and ensure those benchmarks are meaningful to all those involved. Answer the question: Is this a training problem?

Step 3: Design for practice. Stick to your focus, knowing that you can expand learning experiences in future iterations. Test your designs with your target learner population and analyze the feedback. Iterate on your designs to refine the experience. Be prepared to make changes. Don't lose sight of your audience or your objectives when choosing an immersive technology (don't be blinded by "Ooooh! Shiny!").

Step 4: Sell your solution. Even great learning experiences can fail when they have bad press or no marketing. Talk in terms of organizational goals, but frame the learning experience for the individual's benefit.

Step 5: Show your work. Compare training analytics against performance metrics. Identify the gaps and make refinements to close them. Talk the language of the business and communicate your value in terms that make sense to them. Market your successes and learn from things that aren't working. Share your stories so that others may learn from your experience (Bozarth, 2013). In fact, share your experiences with me! You might just be in the next book...www.immersivelearningbook.com.

Your organization might not be prepared for the shift in learning philosophy that comes with changing from traditional instructional design to immersive learning design. Be prepared to answer lots of questions about why and how from executives and management. Tell them that you're focused on improving organizational performance by designing for practice through immersive learning. Share examples from this book to show how other organizations have tackled similar challenges. Your learners might resist participating in a learning experience and claim all they need is some information to get better. Be prepared to challenge that assertion. Explain that you're not interested in what they know, but what they can do. Explain that you want to give them opportunities to practice, not just provide them with resources.

FUTURE STATE

What will the future of learning look like: What role will immersive learning play? Think about how you would train people if you had no limitations. The implications of a completely open opportunity for designing immersive learning experiences can be realized with technologies readily available today. Collaborative learning, social learning, coaching, mentoring, real-time feedback on performance in realistic environments—all of this is possible with learning designed for immersive technologies.

The key, of course, is that this is already possible. It relies on design, and new ways of thinking about instructional design, to enable immersion. Instructional designers, teachers, and higher education faculty will be challenged to think about how to design immersive experiences, which provide opportunities for practice, personalized feedback, and constructivist learning. No longer will traditional e-learning design be acceptable; simulations, games, and social, real-time interactions will be common and expected. Instructional and curriculum design, as practices, will necessarily have to change to accommodate the new possibilities and potential of immersive learning environments.

One of the essential elements of future immersive learning environments will be the integration of social media and opportunities for social learning. Many immersive technologies are by their construct already social, enabling learners to communicate in real time with each other and interact in ways not possible through other technologies.

The shift from single learner experiences to social learning experiences will be one of the benchmarks of effectively designed blended learning solutions in the future.

From the beginning of this book, the focus has been on bridging the gap between knowledge acquisition and behavior change. The "underpants gnomes" were sure that if they just collected enough underpants it would result in profits. Many learning professionals treat the training process the same way, thinking that if they present learners with enough content, their performance will improve. Unfortunately for the underpants gnomes, and organizations, the leap is too great. Practice is the key to improvement, and immersive learning is the best vehicle for scalable practice.

Leave this book thinking of how you would bridge the gap in your organization. Think about the biggest performance issue in your organization. Identify and quantify its impact on the business. Analyze all of the factors contributing to this issue. Then ask, could this issue be improved through practice? Through seeing the issue from a different perspective in the organization? From seeing the long-term impacts of decision making? Then, design an immersive learning solution to address it.

So what does the future of immersive learning look like? It will look very much like the apprenticeship model, but with avatars and characters engaged in immersive practice and learning experiences. Learning communities will engage in real life and immersive technologies interchangeably, with common threads of learning woven together with characters and story line. Most importantly, learners will practice real tasks, debrief with peers, and receive personalized feedback and coaching from mentors or experts. The future of learning through immersive design truly is learning by doing.

REFERENCES

Aldrich, C. (2013). "The Emerging Unifying View of Highly Interactive Virtual Environment Learning." Retrieved on September 17, 2013, from www.clarkaldrichdesigns.com/2009/02/emerging-unifying-view-of-highly.html.

Allen Interactions. (2007). "Rapid Interactive Design for E-Learning Certificate Program." Retrieved on September 18, 2013, from www.instructionaldesign.org/models/addie_weaknesses.html.

Barseghian, T. (2012). "New Survey: Half of Teachers Use Digital Games in Class." MindShift. Retrieved September 18, 2013, from http://blogs.kqed.org/mindshift/2012/05/new-survey-half-of-teachers-use-digital-games-in-class/.

Bean, C. (2011). "Avoiding the Trap of Clicky-Clicky Bling-Bling." eLearn Magazine. Retrieved on September 17, 2013, from http://elearnmag.acm.org/archive.cfm?aid = 1999745.

Bozarth, J. (2013). "Show Your Work." T + D. Retrieved September 18, 2013, from www.astd.org/Publications/Magazines/TD/TD-Archive/2013/05/Show-Your-Work.

DeAngelis, T. (2012). "A Second Life for Practice?" American Psychological Association 43(3): 48.

Dirksen, J. (2010). "Learning Games and Sims—All About the Feedback." LEEF Blog. Retrieved on September 17, 2013, from http://leefblog.com/2010/03/learning-games-and-sims-all-about-the-feedback/.

------. (2011). Design for How People Learn. Berkeley, CA: New Riders.

Donath, J. (2007). "Virtually Trustworthy." Science 317(5834): 53-54.

Dugas, Diana. "Immersive Game Design Document." Term paper for LTMS 531, Harrisburg University, Pennsylvania, 2011.

Echo. (2012). 2012 Global Customer Service Barometer. Retrieved on September 20, 2013, from http://about.americanexpress.com/news/docs/2012x/axp_2012gcsb_us.pdf.

Entertainment Software Association. (2011). Essential Facts About the Computer and Video Game Industry. Retrieved on September 18, 2013, from www.theesa.com/facts/pdfs/ESA_EF_2011.pdf.

Evens, M., and J. Michael. (2005). One-on-One Tutoring By Humans and Computers. Mahweh, NJ: Lawrence Erlbaum Associates, Inc.

References

Fast Company Staff. (2007). "Fast Talk: Getting a (Second) Life." Fast Company. Retrieved on September 17, 2013, from www.fastcompany.com/58460/fast-talk-getting-second-life.

Fox, J., J.N. Bailenson, and T. Ricciardi. (2012). "Physiological Responses to Virtual Selves and Virtual Others." Journal of Cyber Therapy & Rehabilitation 5(1): 69-72.

Gladwell, M. (2011). Outliers: The Story of Success. New York: Hachette Book Group.

Grant Thornton. (2013). Global Economy in 2013: Uncertainty Weighing on Growth. Retrieved on September 27, 2013, from www.internationalbusinessreport.com/files/global%20 economy%20in%202013%20-%20final.pdf.

Henderson, S.J., and S. Feiner. (2009). "Evaluating the Benefits of Augmented Reality for Task Localization in Maintenance of an Armored Personnel Carrier Turret." IEEE International Symposium on Mixed and Augmented Reality. Retrieved September 18, 2013, from http://graphics.cs.columbia.edu/projects/armar/pubs/henderson_feiner_ismar2009.pdf.

Holton, D.L. (2010). How People Learn With Computer Simulations. In Handbook of Research on Human Performance and Instructional Technology, eds., H. Song, and T. Kidd.

Joslin Diabetes Center. (2009). "Behavioral Medicine at Joslin: Resources and Expectations for Affiliated Programs." Retrieved on October 22, 2013, from http://google2.joslin.org/search?q=BehavioralMedicineServiceJoslin&ie=UTF-8&site=Dev-NewSite&output=xml_no_dtd&client=joslin_dotorg&lr=&proxystylesheet=joslin_dot_org&oe=UTF-8&filter=0.

Koster, R. (2004). A Theory of Fun for Game Design. Scottsdale, AZ: Paraglyph Press.

Kraft, P. (2013). "The Power of High Expectations for Students and Schools." Exploring Education. Retrieved on September 18, 2013, from http://blogs.parktudor.org/exploringeducation/2012/10/the-power-of-high-expectations-for-students-and-schools/.

KZero Worldswide. (2013). Industry Forecasts: Virtual Worlds, Virtual Goods, and Augmented Reality Sectors. Retrieved September 20, 2013, from www.kzero.co.uk/.

Lacey, T.A., and B. Wright. (2010). Occupational Employment Projections to 2018. Monthly Labor Review. Retrieved on September 18, 2013, from www.bls.gov/opub/mlr/2009/11/art5full.pdf.

Larsen, C.R. (2009). "Effect of Virtual Reality Training on Laparoscopic Surgery: Randomised Controlled Trial." BMJ 2009: 338.

Markham, J. (2010). "Game Trains Soldiers in a Virtual Iraq or Afghanistan." The University of Texas at Dallas News Center. Retrieved on September 27, 2013, from www.utdallas.edu/news/2010/2/23-1251_Game-Trains-Soldiers-in-a-Virtual-Iraq-or-Afghanis_article.html.

McShane, M., B. Jarrell, S. Nirenburg, G. Fantry, and S. Beale. (2013). Training Clinical Decision Making Using Cognitively Modeled Virtual Patients. National Institutes of Health and National Library of Medicine. Retrieved on September 18, 2013, from http://mastri.umm.edu/NIH-Book/virtual_patient.html.

Nowak, K.L., and C. Rauh. (2006). "The Influence of the Avatar on Online Perceptions of Anthropomorphism, Androgyny, Credibility, Homophily, and Attraction." Journal of Computer-Mediated Communication 11(1): 153-178.

Pfeffer, J. (2000). The Knowing-Doing Gap: How Smart Companies Turn Knowledge Into Action. Boston, MA: Harvard Business School Publishing.

Pink, D. (2011). Drive: The Surprising Truth About What Motivates Us. New York: Riverhead Books.

Quest to Learn. (2013). "About Q2L." Retrieved on September 17, 2013, from http://q2l.org/about.

Quinn, C., and M. Conner. (2005). Engaging Learning: Designing E-Learning Simulation Games. San Francisco, CA: Pfeiffer.

Rollings, A., and D. Morris. (1999). *Game Architecture and Design*. Scottsdale, AZ: Coriolis Group Books.

Schell, J. (2008). The Art of Game Design: A Book of Lenses. Burlington, MA: Elsevier.

Specht, M., S. Ternier, and W. Greller. (2011). "Mobile Augmented Reality for Learning: A Case Study." Journal of the Research Center for Educational Technology (RCET) 7(1): 117-127.

The Coaches Centre. (2012). "About Us." Retrieved on September 27, 2013, from http://thecoachescentre.com/about.jsp.

TrainingIndustry.com. (2013). "Size of Training Industry." Retrieved on September 17, 2013, from www.trainingindustry.com/wiki/entries/size-of-training-industry.aspx.

University of Exeter. (2007). "Why We Learn From Our Mistakes." ScienceDaily. Retrieved August 21, 2013, from www.sciencedaily.com/releases/2007/07/070702084247.htm.

Warburton, S. (2008). "Loving Your Avatar: Identity, Immersion, and Empathy." Liquid Learning. Retrieved on September 17, 2013, from http://warburton.typepad.com/liquidlearning/2008/01/loving-your-ava.html.

White, G. (2009). "Audio Game Maker." Second Life for the Visually Impaired. Retrieved September 17, 2013, from www.blindsecondlife.blogspot.com/.

Wikipedia. (2013). "Reactivity (Psychology)." Retrieved on September 17, 2013, from http://en.wikipedia.org/wiki/Reactivity_(psychology).

Wikipedia. (2013). "Flow (Psychology)." Retrieved on September 18. 2013, from http://en.wikipedia.org/wiki/Flow_(psychology).

Wikipedia. (2013). "Serious Game." Retrieved on September 17, 2013, from http://en.wikipedia.org/wiki/Serious_games.

Yee, N., and J. Bailenson. (2007). "The Proteus Effect: The Effect of Transformed Self-Representation on Behavior." Human Communication Research 33(3): 271-290.

------. (2009). "The Difference Between Being and Seeing: The Relative Contribution of Self-Perception and Priming to Behavioral Changes Via Digital Self-Representation." Media Psychology 12: 2, 195-209.

Zaibak, O. (2010). "20 Customer Service Statistics for 2011." Customer 1. Retrieved on September 20, 2013, from www.customer1.com/blog/customer-service-statistics.

ACKNOWLEDGMENTS

The process of writing this book occurred across relationships ending and beginning, new jobs, and a move across the country. There are so many people to thank for supporting me throughout the journey.

Thank you to Ken Olbrish, who got me started in writing a book (which eventually turned into this book) by transcribing conversations, watching the kiddos to give me time to write, and providing overall moral support. I probably never would have even started without your encouragement and incredibly fast typing.

Thank you to ASTD, but particularly Justin Brusino and Heidi Smith, for pushing and pulling and moving this forward. Justin, thank you for having faith in me to write this book and for giving me the chance. Heidi, thank you for your patience! This process taught me a lot about myself and the writing process, and you both gave me the space, encouragement, and sometimes kick in the butt to continue writing and learning.

Thank you to my professional inspirations. Clark Quinn, your work inspired much of my thinking and design practice, and your feedback on my early drafts was invaluable in helping me think through my thoughts and practices to get them on paper. Karl Kapp, thank you for including me in some of your previous books (mini book projects!), for your great thinking on games, simulations, and virtual worlds, and your much-needed friendship and insight (over some delicious Indian food) to let me know I wasn't alone in my book writing struggles.

Thank you to the serious games industry for continuing to promote best practices, research, and case studies. We're getting to the tipping point! To Richard Smith, Kevin Corti, Michael Fergusson, Dustin Clingman, and many others who play at the intersection of games and learning: Thank you for your good work and examples, for showing

how it can be done, and not just talking about it. Remember when we couldn't even call them games? To the practitioners and authors and experts whom I've had the privilege to meet and chat with in person, and (of course) follow on all the various social media sites—thank you for sharing, and for providing insight and new perspectives: Jesse Schell, Eric Zimmerman, Katie Salen, Raph Koster, Clark Aldrich, Jane McGonigal, Ian Bogost, and James Gee.

Thank you to Harrisburg University, and specifically Andy Petroski, Charles Palmer, and Jen Reiner, who brought me into the fold in helping educate a new generation of designers on how to marry immersive design and learning. I hope to continue working with you all for many, many years to come.

Thank you to my graduate students in the fall of 2011, who helped me refine the curriculum on design practices that is the basis of this book. In particular, thank you to Diana Dugas, whose exceptional examples for design work I used throughout.

Thank you to my Tandem Learning compadres, the original crew: Marcus Hswe, Kristen Cromer, and Jedd Gold. The work that we did, the adventures we had, the memories we shared…how much fun was that? Who said learning can't be fun? I love you all and look forward to our reunion tour.

Thank you to the eLearning Guild for giving a little innovative design company the chance to move the learning industry forward. Thank you especially to Brent Schlenker, who enthusiastically embraced my crazy ideas and let us immerse DevLearn participants in new learning experiences.

Thank you to all of the individuals and companies who gave me permission to feature their work. Thanks especially to Julie Dirksen for your inspiring first book that helped me think about this book differently; to Kevin Thorn and Trina Rimmer for always having examples of REAL WORK that illustrates what many people just talk about; to Cammy Bean for being able to say the right thing in the right way at the right time, and to whom I look to when I need some inspiration to keep going; to Jane Bozarth, who is relentlessly practical and full of life, truly lives learning, and probably finished another book in the time it took me to write these acknowledgments; and to Dan Pink for writing *Drive* and changing the whole way I thought about the impact of motivation and design for immersive learning.

Thank you to Ellen Wagner for keeping practical, meaningful metrics on my mind and amazing "tickly pear" preserves in my pantry. Thank you to Reuben Tozman for your friendship, support, and reminders that no one is as awesome as they pretend to be. Thank you to Kel Smith for always making me feel like I really am a rock star.

Thank you to my mentor and my friend, Kevin Kruse. It was an honor to learn from you and see from your example how to immerse people in learning, helping them work through their failure points, and measuring their improvement and success.

Thank you to Melissa Peterson, who helped wrangle many of the case studies featured in the book, who has designed some brilliant immersive experiences, and to whom I have the privilege to call friend. I'm looking forward to what's next!

To my kiddos, who think it's pretty cool that I have a book they can buy on Amazon, but who have also seen the immense amount of work that it took to get it there.

And finally, to my love, my best friend, my partner, John Pagano, who reminded me who I am. I love our life.

—Koreen Olbrish Pagano

ABOUT THE AUTHOR

Koreen Olbrish Pagano is passionate about helping people learn more effectively. She advocates new ways of using technology for learning, with an emphasis on performance improvement and behavioral change. Always exploring what's next, Koreen believes that each new cool technology should be vetted through the lens of "how can this help people learn?" A designer at heart, her greatest desire is to make the world better through the effective use of new technologies.

Koreen has strong ties to education, having received her MS in Curriculum and Instruction from Penn State University. In 1999, she helped start Freire Charter School in Philadelphia, teaching there for two years before moving back into organizational learning and instructional design with a focus on online leadership simulations. When the dot-com bubble burst, Koreen spent several years designing sales training for companies in the pharmaceutical industry. In 2008, Koreen founded Tandem Learning to demonstrate the untapped potential of immersive learning design. Although technology-agnostic, Koreen specialized in virtual worlds and alternate reality games (ARGs) for learning at Tandem until the company was acquired by Ayogo Games in 2011.

An internationally recognized speaker and organizational consultant, Koreen presents on learning trends, design, and practice for events and organizations. She has taught graduate courses on instructional design and game design at Harrisburg University and writes the blog *Learning in Tandem*. Currently, Koreen is a senior product manager at lynda.com in Carpinteria, California. She lives with her incredible husband, their six amazing kids, and their two little grey dogs with ocean on the left and mountains to the right.

INDEX

Index